COME
BACK TO
JESUS

—AND DON'T BRING
YOUR BLACKBERRY

In "Come Back to Jesus – and Don't Bring your Blackberry" Tanya Logan draws upon the richness of her own Christian experience and exposition of the scripture to provide hope to people who have gotten sidetracked in life by paying more attention to things than to God. She relates how she was able to find the depth of Christian commitment when she was able to "disconnect" from those things that unintentionally and unknowingly become our idols. Her story may be your story. Join her on a trip back to Jesus by re-discovering what He truly means to you.

—Marvin Cameron, D.Min.,
Pastor, First Baptist Church, Kingsport, TN

"Tanya's book, "Come Back to Jesus and Don't bring your Blackberry" pierces right to the heart of our faith. I would recommend it to anyone who is serious about their walk with the Lord."

—Jeff Brooks, Evangelist
President, A Certain Sound

This is a very inspiring, well- written, step by step plan of contemporary Bible study and worship, with the outcome of drawing believers closer to God as disciples of Christ. The book illustrates many of the obstacles and idols that alienate us from having the marvelous relationship with God that is readily available. Our Christian walk is often full of unrecognized detriments to our faith. The author has conveyed her own personal spiritual life hindrances and victories in the resource material. This will be a great foundational resource for individual, bible study groups, or one-on-one studies. The leader's guide enhances the study by equipping the teacher or leader with tools and the design for leading. The leader's guide will help prepare the leader both spiritually and intellectually to connect with the class or students.

Tanya is a very well versed writer and I appreciate knowing that one of our seminary students is involved in such an important ministry of teaching others the Word and how to apply it to their daily lives.

—Dr. Roy Harkness,
Professor, Trinity College of the Bible and Trinity Theological Seminary

COME
BACK TO
JESUS

—AND DON'T BRING
YOUR BLACKBERRY

TANYA LOGAN

WestBow
PRESS
A DIVISION OF THOMAS NELSON

WestBow Press books may be ordered through booksellers or by contacting:

WestBow Press
A Division of Thomas Nelson
1663 Liberty Drive
Bloomington, IN 47403
www.westbowpress.com
1-(866) 928-1240

ISBN: 978-1-4497-8207-8 (sc)
ISBN: 978-1-4497-8206-1 (e)

Library of Congress Control Number: 2013901245

Printed in the United States of America

WestBow Press rev. date: 1/22/2013

Also by Tanya Logan, writing as Tanya R. Davis

The Real Estate Developer's Handbook

How to Be your own Contractor and Save Thousands on your New House or Renovation While Keeping your Day Job

How to Open and Operate a Financially Successful Construction Company

How to Make Thousands at Real Estate Auctions (co-written with Rob Friedman)

For Heath, Amy and Holly.

May you always delight in the Lord.

TABLE OF CONTENTS

PREFACE

When I began this journey, I had no idea how long it might take or where it would lead. I started writing this book in my head in 2003, but it wasn't until 2011 that I finally had the time and resources to sit down and write it out.

Writing for the Lord is always an adventure, and this project was no exception. You spend days in prayer, days in research, and some days lying across the keyboard crying, "Submit! Submit!" Sometimes you can't wait to get started, and sometimes the thing you are writing about is so personal and so deep that it wears you out just to think about it. Occasionally that small voice whispers something specific, like, *Get to your computer and open to Isaiah 55.*

This writing project started as a Christian living book rather than a study. Slowly it dawned on me that Bible studies are what I'm called to do—both to write and teach them. I'm enjoying teaching this manuscript for the second time, even before it goes to print. And I've already started writing a new study on prayer.

My hope is that you find what God intended for you to find within these pages, and that your life in Christ is always an adventure . . .

And my God will meet all your needs according to the riches
of his glory in Christ Jesus. (Philippians 4:19)

Who Is My God?

"The Lord does not look at the things people look at. People look at
the outward appearance, but the Lord looks at the heart."
—1 Samuel 16:7

Do you ever feel like you used to be a lot closer to God than you are now? Do you
wish you could return to that time in your past?

Sarah dreams of the days when she was younger and lived at home. Her father worked,
and her mother stayed home and took care of Sarah and her younger brother. She accepted
Christ at an early age and thoroughly enjoyed their church-centered life—going to church
on Sundays and Wednesdays, wearing her little dresses and carrying her white Bible, and
being greeted by everyone there.

Now Sarah is twenty-seven years old and lives a couple of hours away from her former
hometown, too far to attend church on Sundays. She really hasn't connected with a church in
her area. So far she's still a "visitor" where she goes occasionally, because she hasn't changed
her membership. She only attends once or twice a month and longs for the days when she
felt God was truly in her life.

Jimmy is a married man, although he has not lived with his wife in over two years. He
refuses to file for divorce because he took his vows before God, and that's the way he intends

to keep it. Jimmy, a deacon in his church, came home early one day from work to find his wife with another man. He moved out, and because she was still taking the children to their church, he found another one. But he feels that now he is only going through the motions. Where once God was everything in his life, Jimmy's core has been shaken and he has a lot of questions—and a lot of anger. He tries to hold it in, hoping that one day things will straighten out. He finds himself unable to pray. When he tries, a great wave of anger takes hold. He thinks maybe God has distanced Himself.

Maybe you've never felt that closeness to God at all but you long for it. We're made that way; God created our hearts with a special space that can only be filled up with His presence. So if you don't feel close to Him, of course you will ache for Him.

When I first became a Christian, I was eager to get a lot of head knowledge, so I did a lot of reading, but I'm not sure I truly "got" it. I was very much into the rules, but didn't know a lot about love and grace. One thing I'm sure of now is that I didn't know Jesus as I could have. Part of that was probably my personality and age (fifteen). Part of it was simply that each of us has to mature in our knowledge of Christ and the Bible one step at a time.

Some years later I came to a point where everything that could possibly go wrong did. I was a single mother of three when I became so sick I couldn't even walk. I had little help or support; their dad lived hundreds of miles away. A realtor by profession, it was impossible to show property without the ability to walk—and impossible to sell it without showing it! When it was time to renew my real estate license, I didn't even have the money to pay for it. Fortunately I had bought some rental houses, so by selling them off I barely kept my head above water.

The doctors weren't sure what was wrong with me. All the tests were coming back clear, yet I couldn't walk twenty yards without needing to sit down. My hands were so weak I asked store clerks to tear my checks out of the checkbook. I was constantly sick to my stomach.

When the children left for school, for the first time in my life I was in a silent, empty house. I began spending all those hours of quiet time with my Bible. I prayed, read, and prayed some more. I found Christian forums online and prayed with others. You know what happened? I've never been so close to the Lord as I was during that otherwise awful year. He guided me through slowly; sometimes I felt like I was tiptoeing around a bunch of land mines. In the end, I learned to manage what turned out to be a chronic illnesses and food allergies, and I changed professions to something that let allowed more control over my schedule. I also got rid of not just one bad relationship but everyone who was toxic in my life. Most of all, I developed a rich, deep closeness with the Lord.

So if you asked me that first question, "Has there ever been a time when you felt closer to God than you do now?" I would have to say my Year of Illness and Uncertainty.

Do you have a special time like that? List it here: _____

Now I'd like to ask you a personal question. Have you ever let something take over your time so much that it caused you not to do things you normally would or should do? For example, you let your laundry slide, or the house went dirty for two weeks, or your entire routine changed? I'm not talking about when the family got a new puppy or you broke your leg. I'm talking about ongoing activities or interests, things that we laughingly say we are "obsessed with." Mine is making beaded jewelry. If I don't exercise a lot of self-discipline, the house gets cluttered, or dinner doesn't get made because I "just have to" work on some new piece of jewelry. I can't quit until it's done. For some it might be surfing the Internet or watching movie marathons.

Write your "obsession" here: _____

One of the reasons we often fail to have a good relationship with the Lord is because we allow other "stuff" to get in the way. These things are time-stealers. They suck up our day, over and over, so that we said, "I want to spend more time with God" yesterday . . . last week . . . last month . . . until suddenly it's been years.

Sometimes these things that get in the way of our worship become so huge in our lives that they are like idols or gods (with a little g). Some people call them *functional* gods or *false* gods. Others call them addictions or obsessions. If you don't like one of these terms, feel free to call them something else. Does that sound like a giant leap, from having something that sucks your time away to worshiping an idol? If it does, consider my working definition of an idol: *anything that repeatedly gets between you and your worship of God.* The thing—the one ultimate thing that drives you, that *repeatedly* gets between you and your worship of God— that's your time-stealer. It usually is not a bad thing on its own, but elevating it onto a pedestal makes it a problem. For example:

If you're doing it in place of spending time with your child, it's an idol.

If you're doing it out of fear or reverence *and it's not God*, it's an idol.

If you trust or love or obey him more than anything on earth or in heaven, he's an idol.

Through the next six weeks, we're going to uncover these time-stealers, see how they can wreak havoc with our spiritual well-being, examine how some of them can become idols, and discover ways to make sure they don't get in the way again. It's always difficult to balance our spiritual health with the rest of the things in our life—work, family, other obligations, etc. Sometimes it seems like your life is driving you, instead of the other way around. Many of us have asked the question, "Lord, I know I'm supposed to spend time with You—but how?" Hopefully by the end of this study you will not only understand how but also be well on your way to creating the spiritual life you want in Jesus Christ.

When I first had the idea for this book, I asked a group of women what they thought might get in the way of their worship. Here are a few of the things they said.

My house, money, my car—materialism. This is a common and easy trap to fall into. I believe that the media, especially reality TV shows, are at fault. There are of course other reasons to become materialistic—but in a certain sense, you can't want it if you don't know it exists.

Twitter, Facebook, my computer, my phone—social connections. There are two problems with this particular time-stealer. One is the amount of time they take away from your family or your relationship with God. The other is that if you are communicating with strangers on the Internet, you really aren't connecting at all. It's a fallacy. Later in this study, I'll ask you to give up some of these. Don't worry, it won't be too painful!

Fear, jealousy, pride, perfectionism—feelings. I knew someone whose counselor kept telling her, "Feelings are not facts." I sided with my friend, of course, thinking that they are, if you're the one feeling them. As I studied this issue more, however, I began to understand. Feelings *seem* to be facts while you're having them. They feel very real. But later your feelings can change. You might learn more about a situation, or you might have an attitude adjustment—and the feelings are no longer present. King Saul had feelings of jealousy that were so great they drove him to be obsessed with killing David—his successor to the throne! I would guess that Saul thought his feelings were indeed facts, though they were not based on anything David had actually done to Saul.

Would it have ever occurred to you to think of Facebook, your new phone, or your fancy car as an idol? If not, can you at least agree that these are time-stealers? So many little functional gods run around in our lives. In a sense we're uneducated about them, and therefore unable to recognize their presence in our lives or the lives of our friends. Because we are not sensitive to the way these gods form from something seemingly innocent, we don't know how to handle them when they crop up. So we allow them to take over. We may still worship God, but we serve another. Look over at the person who is texting in church and consider whether her obsession is blocking her worship of God.

As you read the examples of time-stealers/idols above, do you recognize any functional or false gods of your own? _____

Write them here. _____

Let's be clear here. I don't have to crave evil to make something into an idol. I don't have to *be* evil either. We can be good people who want a good thing and still become idolaters. We can want it for a very good reason. The thing is not the problem. Rather one's own desire for that thing becomes misshapen. Good desire goes awry. The thing you wanted then becomes an idol, elevated to a status higher than other people or things around you. Higher than Christ.

The internal change is extreme. Your heart suddenly feels as if it's bursting with the desire. You're obsessive. You've "got to have it." Now. I can promise you that whether they mention it or not, people around you do see the change in you.

Day 1: Idolatry at Work

Let's take a look for a moment at someone in the Bible who allowed an idol to creep in. The story is found in Luke 12:16–21. Please take a moment to read it now.

Jesus tells of the rich man who built bigger barns and saved back all his grain for retirement. Then he died that night. . . .

> "That's what happens when you fill your barn with Self and not with God."
> (v. 21 MSG)

This story at first glance doesn't seem clear. Why not save for retirement—isn't that what we all do? (I can't help but notice Jesus knew that in the twenty-first century we would totally understand *saving for retirement*.)

But the next verse tells us the real meaning behind the parable: "That's what happens when you fill your barn with Self and not with God."

Aha! The man didn't just save up for retirement; he obsessed over his fortune in grain.

Today we might have a fortune in gold or stocks. Back then grain was like gold. He had tons! He probably sat in the barn and sifted it through his fingers, crowing to himself as the cool grain ran through his hands. He was so excited about his grain that he built more barns for it. He selfishly kept everything. No feeding the widows as was the custom, no sharing with the children or the neighbors. It was like winning the lottery—he was set for life.

Somewhere along the way he forgot about God. He slowly stopped praying and sacrificing. He was no longer seen at the temple or holiday gatherings. He was too busy working on the fortune he'd amassed.

That's exactly what happens to us when idols creep in. We gradually give up the life we had in Christ. The morning Bible study slips from five days a week to three to two. We start skipping evening services, and nobody really says anything, so we skip a Sunday morning or two, even though we've gone to church every Sunday all our lives. As we become more involved with our idol, we find that skipping church doesn't really hurt so much, and hey, what did we really have in common with those folks anyway? Sadly they don't usually call to check on us. This only reinforces our lack of closeness with fellow church members. Plus, now that we aren't in church on Sunday mornings, we see lots of other people who aren't in church either. *I'm in good company*, you say to yourself. By now we're well on our way to being idol worshipers. The problem is, we don't recognize it.

Let's look further in Luke to see what God's Word suggests we do to keep from becoming like the grain gatherer:

> "What I'm trying to do here is get you to relax, not be so preoccupied with getting so you can respond to God's giving. . . . Steep yourself in God-reality, God-initiative, God-provisions. You'll find all your everyday human concerns will be met. Don't be afraid of missing out. . . . Be generous. Give to the poor. Get yourselves a bank that can't go bankrupt. . . . The place where your treasure is, is the place you will most want to be, and *end up being.*" (Luke 12:29–34 MSG, emphasis added)

The place where your treasure is. That's where you are. Whether on the couch in front of the TV, remote firmly in hand, or logging onto Facebook just one more time before bed, or—like me—sitting at a desk making jewelry—if you do it to excess, that's your treasure. The place where you will end up being.

Now, think about ending up, or more correctly arriving at "the end." Do you really want to spend eternity sitting in front of a great big TV screen, computer, or pile of beads instead of in heaven in the presence of God? Honestly none of us want to do that forever. Going to heaven is more important than any show, exercise class, ball game, or other earthly activity. Setting our sights on heaven is what Paul meant when he wrote, "I press on toward the goal to win the prize for which God has called me heavenward in Christ Jesus" (Philippians 3:14).

Many people are uncomfortable thinking about having idols or false gods. They feel they can't relate to them. So I suggest to understand it better, we might need to change its name to *idealizing*. What is your ideal? It could be a certain lifestyle, a house, living in a particular neighborhood, marrying a certain type of person, having a particular job. The list could go on forever.

Write your ideal here: _____

I first presented this study with a small focus group made up of my own Christian friends. You would not look at this group and think of them as having any false or functional gods. But through the study, each woman (and two men) found, if not a full-fledged god, at least a time-stealer, an adjustment that needed to be made in order to have a better spiritual life. Some found they needed to reach out to others more, some had to put aside fiction in order to stay in the Word, and one gave up golf time—well, part of it—to spend more time with her husband.

I myself have worked on this book for a year. During that time the Lord has worked on me in so many ways. I can't believe one person needed so much work! I've given up hobby time and TV time. I didn't make any jewelry at all from December to April. I put an audio version of the Bible on my iPod and continue to listen to it every night at bedtime instead of music, in addition to my morning studies. I installed a Bible app on my iPhone, which I now read when I'm standing in line or waiting for an appointment. He has saturated me in the Word.

Let's have a look at 1 Samuel, a book we probably don't spend a lot of time in. I know I don't. It's full of war and death, and most of the characters use a sword to kill every single person they come across. Not my kind of reading, really.

In the book of 1 Samuel, God accuses Samuel of moping around over Saul, and tells him that Saul is simply no longer going to be Israel's king—no matter how much Samuel whines. Instead God has already chosen a different king. He sends Samuel to gather a group of people and lead them in worship, and says He will point out which person should be anointed. It's someone from Jesse's family, but that's all Samuel knows when he arrives. So he tries to guess which of Jesse's sons will be the new king, but God says:

"God judges persons differently than humans do. Men and women look at the face; God looks into the heart." (1 Samuel 16:7 MSG)

So Jesse presented each one of his sons, and Samuel explained seven times that God had not chosen that one. Finally he asked Jesse, "Are there no more sons?" There was one more, the sheepherder. Jesse referred to him as the runt. But as we know, David was the one destined to become king, and instantly became filled with the Spirit of God. Perhaps he was small in stature, but he was mighty through the Holy Spirit.

As they grew older, Saul became extremely jealous of David. He chased him all over the country, literally trying to kill him. Saul was single-minded in his obsession to kill David. David mocked him, and in 1 Samuel 26:20 he said, "The King of Israel obsessed with a single flea!"

Saul definitely had an obsession. The thing that was driving him was jealousy, his idol. He was the king after all, with everything at his disposal, every person bowing at his feet. But it wasn't good enough—he wanted to get rid of David. Isn't it interesting that many of us do not consider the Old Testament relevant, yet Saul's jealousy drives home the reality that we are just like the people of that time. How many of us today are driven by an emotion like jealousy, anger, or fear? I'm willing to bet that if we would admit it, many of us are.

On a scale of 1 to 10, how much jealousy (or anger, or other emotion) have you carried in your life?

1☐ 2☐ 3☐ 4☐ 5☐ 6☐ 7☐ 8☐ 9☐ 10☐

_____

Contemplate how this impacted your spiritual life. Write down any reflections you have.

_____

Are you having any anger, jealousy, or strong emotions now that need to be dealt with? If so, what are they?

_____

Take those concerns to God and ask Him to help you deal with them this week.

Day 2: Where We Find Little Gods

MANY PEOPLE, WHEN THEY HEAR the word *idolatry*, think of a deep jungle with strangely painted warriors dancing around a fire . . . then the camera zooms in on an angry, stone-faced image, the idol. We don't usually think of idolaters as those dressed up in Sunday finery sitting on a pew. But there we are.

While it's true that we may not have a problem anymore with worshiping stone images or dancing around fires, we do have difficulty when it comes to money, cars, sports, and many other things. The quandary is that the ones most dangerous to us, which poison us, are difficult to detect. So difficult that almost nobody believes they have an idol, yet almost everybody does.

> The eyes of the Lord are everywhere, keeping watch on the wicked and the good. (Proverbs 15:3)

Nothing is hidden. The heart thoughts are laid bare for Him to observe. To the Lord, we may look just like those bushmen dancing around the fire.

Idols, or false gods, can come at us from almost any side. They can be things we crave or desire, like fame or academic success. They can be things missing in our lives, like relationships, money, body image, or status. Sometimes we create them, or at least help elevate them. Fashion idols, political idols, a show called *American Idol* where we *make idols*. We worship them via television, Twitter, newspaper or magazine articles, and Facebook. As a country, we have a hunger to idolize.

Guess what—this is what it's like to be human. Congratulations, we're all normal. But when we allow these idols to permeate our lives, when they get to take over and function as gods, we block our own ability to communicate with the One who should be Lord of our lives. Then we're in spiritual trouble.

Yesterday we looked at Saul's—and our own—jealousy. Idols generally come down to emotions and feelings. Our idol is the thing, the one ultimate thing that drives us to a particular behavior over and over again. And most importantly, idols are the things that keep us away from God.

Idolatry is one of the most discussed problems in the Bible. Yet today's Christians consider it stiff and old-fashioned. We skip over the "idol" verses. After all, we saw the movie

The 10 Commandments, and that's not what we're doing. We dismiss idolatry as something that used to be, that is no more.

Think of carbon dioxide (CO2) for a moment, an invisible yet toxic gas. It can sneak into your system without you knowing it. When CO2 enters the bloodstream, it prevents the body from being able to take in oxygen—which we must have in order to live. CO2 can poison you. That's how these idols work; they sneak in and poison your spiritual life. CO2 also displaces oxygen (O2)—just as idols can displace God.

So the commandment that seemed least relevant becomes the one that is most relevant of all. Yet we avoid it. We ignore it or simply don't see it in our lives and what it does to us. The second commandment says, "You shall not make for yourself an image in the form of anything in heaven above or on the earth beneath or in the waters below" (Exodus 20:3). In Exodus 34:17, it's simplified even further: "Do not make any idols."

We not only make them, we allow them to control us. And when our hearts are controlled by something other than God, everything that comes our way, things that would normally be viewed as opportunities, will be viewed as endless hassles and annoyance. Instead of seeing a needy neighbor as a chance to show mercy, we feel frustrated knowing we'll miss an episode of a favorite TV show. Instead of putting money in the offering plate, we hold back a few dollars to save up for that designer handbag or a new sports car. Or instead of going to church, we stay in bed.

So what is it that drives us to create these obsessions anyway?

Let's look in Deuteronomy. In the first three chapters of this book, Moses has reminded the people that they are God's chosen flock. He outlined for them all the different places they've been, the challenges they've faced, the victories they've won—all because they belong to God.

Please take a moment to read Deuteronomy 4.

In chapter 4, Moses tells them who their God is. Israel's God is different from the gods of all the nations surrounding them because He is not made of wood, stone, or precious metal. Unlike those idols, God can interact with them, speak to them, and tell them what He wants them to do. In verses 15–16, Moses says,

> "You saw no form of any kind the day the Lord spoke to you at Horeb out of the fire. Therefore watch yourselves very carefully, so that you do not become corrupt and make for yourselves an idol, an image of any shape."

Do not become corrupt. Do not make an idol. The Israelites knew the rules, yet they broke them.

So do we. If we know not to do break the laws of God, why do we keep creating idols?

Write your thoughts about this question here: _____

_____

Most times we fall into idol creation rather innocently. It sneaks up on us. It begins as desire and ends up as misshapen longings. During the process of wanting, our want becomes warped. Let's see how.

Sam, an energetic, young go-getter, has a new job. Because she wants to do it well, she begins to work more and more hours until work is the prevalent thing in her life. She lives, breathes, and talks constantly about work. Friendships and other relationships outside of the office fall by the wayside, and her new friends at the new job become the mainstay. She regales her boyfriend with stories from work until he's just sick of it. She forgets to ask him how he's doing. He keeps quiet, seeing that she's just not that interested right now anyway.

Sam can rationalize it—"It's only for a little while, it's what I have to do right now. This is the best thing I can do for my family/career/future." But God is no longer glorified. Something else (her job) has taken over. She is working sixty or more hours a week, and worship has taken a backseat, along with everything else in her life.

It's just for now, she reasons. But how many workaholics have said that early in a career, only to find they're still grinding away six, ten, and twenty-five years later?

This example is perhaps a little oversimplified, but it's how we allow other gods to take over our lives. Remember, the one ultimate thing that drives you is your functional god. If it repeatedly gets between you and your worship of God, it is an idol.

As another example, let's take our American love of sports. Suppose Paul and the other apostles arrived at a coliseum in some big city today. Thousands of stadium seats, megawatts of lighting, TV and radio coverage, fans no matter what the weather. They'd think they were at a religious event, right? I hate to imagine their surprise at the fact that we're putting all that time, energy, effort, and money into a mere sports event—and then we can't show up for church tomorrow morning of course, because we're too tired.

Sam accidentally let a false god take over. It was almost, and only almost, an innocent way of getting into it. We are not totally innocent, because we have choices. And we've made at least one choice, usually several choices, along the way. Sam did. You can be sure she saw at least once or twice that she needed to cut back her hours, that she needed to rearrange her priorities.

There are always signs, incidents when the still, small voice reminds us we're on the wrong path. If we've surrounded ourselves deliberately with the right kind of friends, there could even be face-to-face intervention. Often we ignore it.

Sometimes we are led into idolatry by a friend, relative, or neighbor. It's cool, in style, or will get us into a certain circle. This kind is so much harder to break free from because it involves also breaking from a group of friends.

Alyssa loved to ride horses when she was in college. A few years later, working and living in a new area, she discovered a group of horse lovers who lived near her. "It was so cool," she remembers. "People would just ride right up into the yard, asking if I wanted to ride with them."

The new crowd showed Alyssa lots of nearby trails, and she got to ride more than ever in her life. But the riders used rough language and clearly were not Christians. The big rides were always on Sundays, so she had to make a choice between riding and church. When Alyssa tried to invite one of the women to church, she responded, "Or we could just kick back and have a beer."

Regretfully Alyssa let go of her riding friends. When she did, she found that she'd also let go of a lifestyle. No one came by to ride, so what little riding she did was alone. Since those friends were gone, she had no one to talk to about horses or where to get the best hay or what's new in saddles. Riding alone was lonely. Eventually Alyssa realized it had been months since she had ridden outside her own fields. She ended up selling her horse and moving to town.

Were you waiting for the happy ending? There wasn't an immediate one. Alyssa wasn't thrilled with the change, but she did feel satisfied in knowing she had done the right thing. A year later she had developed friendships that were more real, with other like-minded Christians. She joined a social group that was active and fun. Looking back, she was happy with her decision to let go of her former riding friends—and even her horse.

Sometimes we like something so much it becomes an obsession. Bodybuilding is one activity that immediately comes to mind. I've known several bodybuilders who were so obsessed they let it take over their lives—and in one case, a marriage. Bodybuilding requires a tremendous amount of time, planning, and discipline. It requires a special diet. And I suspect that it makes one extremely competitive, even if when not entering competitions, as there's probably always someone at the gym who is bigger, more sculpted, or can lift more weight.

A bodybuilder can become so obsessed with the sport that it's no longer a sport; it is *him or her*, a way of life, the center of living. A perfect example of an idol.

Another obsession that's rampant in the United States is viewing porn. Think it doesn't exist in the church? Think again. At least 50 percent of Christian men have viewed porn recently.[1] Casual viewers quickly end up becoming obsessed. This puts them into isolation, so they can view their porn almost every waking hour. People who watch porn spend tons of money on it. (Did you know that even online they have to pay to see it? I didn't.) They think it is a "safe" obsession because no one gets hurt.

The problem is, someone does get hurt—you, the porn watcher. Scripture calls you a slave. It's a downward spiral—soft porn leads to hard porn leads to harder porn. If you have a spouse, it's eventually going to deeply hurt your spouse. And porn leads to so much more sin.

Whatever your obsession or addiction, it is always from Satan, and always takes away from God. Christ does not have full reign over everything if we're blocking His power by these obsessions, gods, and idols. We remain open to temptation and unprotected from the onslaught.

"But how can my (insert your obsession here) be from Satan?" you ask. I'm going to use my beaded jewelry as an example. Making jewelry is a hobby. Nothing is wrong with enjoying creating beautiful jewelry. God made me with a double dose of creativity. I like designing it and putting the pieces together, and the whole process is much more important to me than showing it off later. So far, so good.

Then you see reality. My family's dinner was an hour late because I was beading. I could have finished writing the chapter by the deadline, but I didn't because there were "just a few more rows to go." I was exhausted because I stayed up until 2 a.m. finishing those few rows, which were more like thirty and which I had to rip out and redo twice. Then I'm much too exhausted to do the laundry, which is piling up, and too tired to read my Bible lately too. See the obsession creeping in?

Did these examples trigger any thoughts? Write them here: _____

_____

Day 3: Why Deal with Our Idols

SOME MAY WONDER WHY IT matters at all whether we have a time-stealer in our lives or not. *After all, I still attend church on Sunday morning*, we reason. *I still sing in the choir. I dutifully read the Bible according to my prescribed schedule.*

Let's say you want to buy a bigger house. It's a much bigger house than you have now, and you *really* want it. The time you spend daydreaming about it doesn't matter, you insist, because you do all the "right" things. But gradually you become obsessed with buying that house. Your husband argues that there is no way the budget can handle it, but when one comes on the market that fits your criteria, you insist on buying it. Your somewhat harmless daydream became an obsession, then a compulsion. Now your budget, your children, and probably your marriage are in jeopardy.

Our time-stealers don't have to be an explicit rejection of God, but by not dealing with idols, we block our own ability to hear God's voice. We pray with an agenda and expect the answer to reflect those desires. But the agenda is our own, so it won't work. Worse yet, when we aren't listening to God, we can so easily be led into deception—deeper into idol territory, deeper into terrible sin and a dark abyss where God does not approach us at all.

> For this you know with certainty, that no immoral or impure person or covetous man, *who is an idolater*, has an inheritance in the kingdom of Christ and God. (Ephesians 5:5 NASB, emphasis added)

Right there's the problem, and the reason I wrote this study. The presence of an idol removes us from Christ's presence. Because of the idol, we drift from God (see week 2 to come). We fail to delight in Him, and trust me, He fails to delight in us at that moment. Suddenly we're infatuated with *it*, the thing we're obsessing over. It takes over our thoughts, our time. It changes what we do and how we do it. We rush through our daily Bible study or skip it altogether. We pray but drift off, or we haven't prayed in months.

We are blind to the roadblock the false gods create in our worship lives. We can't see *Satan winning in our own Christian lives* through the use of our favorite toys. My prayer is that this study will help make them more visible to each reader.

I read once about people who panned for gold in the Yukon. Just getting to the area was difficult. Supplies had to be moved in stages. Many would-be prospectors didn't make it through the passes. Once there, the weather was brutal; winter often lasted up to eight months. The gold was present as tiny flakes or nuggets in the river bed, so the miners had to get in the water and dig—for fourteen hours a day. This was in the late 1800s, so there were no warm showers waiting afterward, nor was there any heavy equipment to make the job easier. Instead they used their hands and rinsed the rocks in a sieve or a sluice, searching for the flakes. Often the water was frozen, so they had to save the rock, not knowing whether it contained gold.

Many people from the US stampeded to the Yukon area with a desire to make their fortune. Those who did make it lived in dangerous shantytown conditions, subject to epidemics and fire, and those who survived rarely returned home with a fortune. Many left the Yukon to chase the next gold rush . . . and the next . . . Becoming obsessed in their quest for gold, they died in poverty.

When we allow idols to take over, the honor due to God and God only is given away to some part of His creation: a person, place, or thing. One faithful Christian confided that when he had "reading time," he carried not only his Bible but also his current piece of fiction to his chair. One day he realized that he hurried through the Bible reading in order to get to the next chapter of his book. He started taking only the Bible for reading time and began to get more from his reading time with God.

Recognizing any problem is the first step in being able to guard against it. By learning to recognize idols, we can stop them from overtaking our lives.

Even religion can become a functional god, if we are doing it for the wrong reason. When we attempt to live by our own religious plans and projects, we are cut off from Christ. If we seek power in the church for power's sake, we are working under our own plan. But as we remove the idols, we draw nearer to Him and are able to carry out His plans for us. And His plans are always so much better, wiser, and more thorough than anything we could have planned!

All we are, when you get right down to it, is sinners. We have sinful cravings—we're made that way. Our hearts tend to wander. If we let them, they wander on over to something that will pull a little more and a little harder on our fragile grip on the edge of Christ's robe. If we aren't careful, we'll lose that grip altogether. Again, it isn't the "thing" that is bad, but rather our attitude toward it.

It may not seem important to you that you spend a couple of hours a day on Facebook, or that you watch twenty-eight hours of television per week, the national average. Likewise, it's fine to love your dog, exercising, or your hobby. But how many hours do you spend in prayer or worship? Is that time comparable or less? Was there a time in your life when you spent significantly more time in prayer and worship? If so, can you determine what happened to change that? (A test at the end of this week will help you flesh out these answers more fully.)

Please don't mistake my words. I'm not suggesting that Christians should not have fun. I have tons of fun! David had fun—he danced. Jesus was apparently a fun guy, the sort of person others invited to parties and weddings. We just have to be careful of the kind of fun we're having, and whether it is secondary to the responsibilities and relationship with God we already have.

Read Ecclesiastes 9:7–10. If you can, read it in several versions. What part of this reading gives you comfort? _____

So it isn't about being a stick-in-the-mud. Rather it's about responsibility. When we became Christians, we agreed to pursue the things over which Christ presides. We made a promise not to become absorbed with the things all around us but to be alert to Jesus' point of view and where He is acting in our lives.

Please read Colossians 3:5–11

Comments: _____

Having a functional god prevents us from being renewed in the image of the Creator. We can't! We're too busy bowing down in the wrong direction.

Worshiping a false god is a lot like having an addiction. Here is one definition of addiction: "the state of being enslaved to a habit or practice or to something that is psychologically or physically habit- forming, as narcotics, to such an extent that its cessation causes severe trauma."[2] That's probably the one we are most familiar with. Let's say the addiction is alcohol. The Bible tells us that drunkards will not inherit the kingdom of heaven. I feel sure we can extend this addiction to other things like gluttony and drugs.

We could say false gods cause us to do something habitually or compulsively. But God is the only thing we should occupy ourselves with habitually. To do anything else draws us away from Him. He alone is worthy of our complete devotion, love, and service, as Jesus explained in Matthew: "Love the Lord your God with all your heart and with all your soul and with all your mind. This is the first and greatest commandment" (Matthew 22:37).

So if we find ourselves convinced by God through our prayer and Bible study time of being consumed by an idol's presence in our lives, it is up to us to take action. In order to continue as the *new self,* the old stuff must be thrown out.

Often we can't discern this ourselves. We can see it in someone else, of course. Boy, we can't wait to tell somebody what we've just read in the Bible and how it applies to *her* life! But it's so much more difficult to see what is in our own heart and life.

First John 4:8 tells us, "The one who does not love does not know God, for God is love" (NASB). No wonder it's so hard to move these heavy idols. Without the love of God, we can't do it. We must know God, then He will help us to remove the stuff from our lives.

While I was working on this book, a man who holds a church leadership position—who I know watches a lot of television—waved his hands in disgust as I explained my definition of an idol. (An idol is *anything that repeatedly gets between you and your worship of God.*) He wasn't having any of it. Now, I happen to know part of that response was his reaction to a woman telling a man he might be doing something wrong. But more of it was that uncomfortable feeling we get when we know we are hearing that *we need to change.* He was probably imagining having to click off that TV. Change is hard. It's much easier to wave it away, to avoid looking deeply, than to actually move in some other direction. Even if we know we need to make that move.

Please read Psalm 1:1–2 (NASB).

It may seem like a huge leap from watching a little TV or talking to friends on Facebook to "walk[ing] in the counsel of the wicked." but I'm here to tell you that's exactly what we're doing if we do not follow the second part of this passage: delight . . . in the law of the Lord; and in His law *he meditates day and night"*(emphasis added). Would you please mark that in your Bible?

One of the most damaging things Satan does when we've replaced our God-shaped space with something else is mess with our Christian friends. An idol can and often will remove us from friendships. Because we put our time into money, the computer, sports, or whatever our favorite has become, we no longer "need" Christian friends. They seem petty and uptight. The new online friends, for example, seem so much more fun. Our relationships and family life suffer as we allow the idol to slowly take over. Life becomes skewed in favor of the object of our obsession.

I believe God intended for us to have relationships, real relationships that go deep and include the grit of who we really are. He means for us to have relationships with family, friends, church members, and people we see occasionally when we're out. He means for us to develop those relationships much like the one we have developed with Him. When we have an idol, these relationships are the first things that slip. By letting ourselves become double-minded—trying to love our friends/family as well as our idol—we cause those relationships to suffer.

Day 4: God's Instructions

God is Spirit, so He wants us to worship Him with our spirit. Please read John 4:23.

Comments: _____

Do you long to be a true worshiper, as mentioned here? I do. That's why it is so important to me to drive out anything that would get in the way.

Real worship engages the spirit in the pursuit of truth. God is looking for those who are clearly being their authentic selves when they come before him and worship, no matter where they are. Authenticity is far more important than the way we dress, which church we attend, which songs we choose, or what methods we use to express our adoration of Him. Those things don't matter to God. If we intend them as worship, He sees it as such. Authenticity is our soul truth laid bare.

Our God is much more than heathen gods made of stone or metal. He is much more than a human being or nature. He is not like the pantheistic god of the Hindus. He is unlike any other god.

Please read Psalm 135:15–18.

Note that the people who worship the idols will *be like them*! What do you think that means?

_____

Our God is unlimited. John 4:23, which we read earlier, is part of a bigger story, where Jesus was talking with a Samaritan woman. That in itself was an anomaly because Jews didn't talk with Samaritans. But the woman had a question for Him about the proper place to worship. She mentioned that her ancestors had worshiped on a mountain. Because God is a living spirit who loves and communicates with all of us, He is not restricted to being worshiped in only one place. This was a change Jesus told the Samaritan woman about, and a change He was about to reveal to the minds of everyone on earth. No longer do we have to go to a special place to conduct our worship. God is omnipresent—present everywhere.

Do you have a special place where you spend the majority of your worship time? _____

Do you find yourself able to worship everywhere? _____

Why or why not? _____

My tendency is to tell you how to run your life. I use the word *should* a lot. Give me enough time, and I will not only tell you what to do, I'll put it in order and number it for you. I'm not kidding.

A college professor told me a story about teaching teachers how to teach. One of the exercises in her class is write out instructions on how to make popcorn in a microwave oven. What they learned from this exercise is how to give instruction more completely, because typically they forgot to mention a step like, "Pick up the popcorn" or "Open the bag." They had to learn how to put things in order so that another person could follow their instructions to the letter.

But that's not God's way. He doesn't shake His finger and say, "Do this." His book isn't written out in numerical order—like mine. Rather the Bible tells us stories, stories about people. It says, "Here is what it is like to evolve and mature as a human." We see our own stories lived out in other people's lives. We see our mistakes and sins and failings in them.

From the parable in Luke 12 that we read on day 1 this week, we saw that hanging onto our possessions with both hands in a death grip is not what God wants us to do. The writer then explains exactly what we are to do, "Steep yourself in God-reality, God-initiative, God-provisions" (v. 31, MSG).

Steep yourself in God-reality. Make a decision to read— really read—your Bible. Spend time in it every day. There is no one in this world who did not grow closer to God by reading her Bible, but there are plenty who grew further away by not reading it.

There are many ways to read, and many suggestions for how to read your Bible—such as, read it in a different translation than the one you usually read. I also recommend an excellent book that explains a lot about reading the Bible with understanding. It is called *Living By the Book: The Art and Science of Reading the Bible* by William and Howard Hendricks. I keep it on my Kindle and reread it from time to time, to remind myself of different ways to see passages in a new light.

How could you spend more time in the Bible this week?_____

Do you need to set a time in order to do it? _____

Write your Bible reading time here: _____

Steep yourself in God-initiative. One definition of initiative is "one's personal, responsible decision."[3] Make the decision to become God-centered. There are many ways to practice being in God's presence. I invite you to search for them and find the ways that suit you best.

How do you most enjoy being in God's presence? _____

If you aren't sure, explore some ways this week. A few ideas: alone at your desk or in a special quiet place reserved for worship, when you're in the Word, while singing or listening to worship music, in church, outdoors. in your car as you commute to work.

The other half of becoming God-initiated is by choosing to be your best self.

Please read 1 Peter 2:1.

Rid yourselves of _____

By tossing aside sin and choosing to go the other direction, we are more open to the Lord's voice when He speaks. We choose to go the right way and will be rewarded for it.

This is one of the hardest things to do as spiritual people who live daily and interact in the physical world. We have to change the way we act, react, and interact. We are physical beings and have all the desires that go along with that. This sort of change will not come easily to some, especially since it takes a very long time to truly master it. It's about learning to put the spiritual first and the physical second—all the time.

Steep yourself in God-provisions. God meets our needs. He provides us with the Holy Spirit to guide us. He gives us all our physical requirements. He gives us opportunities to obey Him. Use the provisions He has given you so that you can benefit from His love. Be faithful in your attendance to the church to which He has led you. Remember that we are the ones who benefit from our Bible classes, prayers, worship services, giving, and songs of praise. We grow spiritually when we are doing spiritual things.

If you cannot see the provisions right now that God has given you recently, ask Him to open your eyes so that you are able to recognize and acknowledge them. Thank Him for His wonderful gifts.

In obeying the gospel through salvation, you acknowledged Jesus as both Lord and Christ (see Acts 2:36). Therefore obey His commandments. That includes the last sentence from 2 Timothy 3:1–5.

Please read the verses, and write the last sentence here: _____

_____

Are you strong enough to do that? _____

Why or why not? _____

Day 5: Difficult Questions

THESE ARE QUESTIONS TO ASK yourself, without sharing the answers with anyone around you. Think carefully and deeply about each one.

1. **Who is my God?**

To answer this, take a long look at yourself and your life and consider these questions:
   » Where do you spend your time?
   » Where you spend your disposable income?
   » Where do you turn when your emotions go out of control?

2. **Sin**

Most of us are not guilty of every sin in the book. Rather we tend to repeat the same two or three sins over and over. With that in mind:
   » What are your sins?
   » When does sin tend to happen for you?
   » Is there a reason, a person that is usually present, or a trigger? (Be careful here. We're not trying to find someone to blame. We're trying to take ownership and move the sin out of our lives.)

> » What one item do you need to remove or get under control today in order to not be in the grip of idols?

3. Influence

Are you having a positive impact on the world around you, or are you stopped because of sin, worldliness, etc.?

4. Time

How much time do you spend with the Lord every day? (This can be Bible reading, prayer, or even listening to praise music.)

Now list five other activities you spend time on, and the amount of time you spend on those. You may need to keep a time log for a few days to calculate it.

1. _____

2. _____

3. _____

4. _____

5. _____

Are there things you need to let go of in order to honor Jesus? It's up to us to witness to the lost, and we can't do it if we're too busy playing the same video game for the twenty-sixth time. If we are steeped in the things of God, though—God-reality, God-provisions, and God-initiative—we witness to those around us without ever saying a word. Instead it shows through the lives we live.

Lord, as I go about my work this week, please make me mindful of the false gods I embrace. Open my eyes to see where I can improve so I will serve you better. Amen.

Seduced by the World

Reach out to the homeless and loveless in their plight, and
guard against corruption from the godless world.
—James 1:27 (MSG)

Day 1: Drifting

THE GOSPEL OF JESUS CHRIST is hands down the most encouraging book ever written for man. Through the gospel, we learn how to be forgiven for the things we've done wrong; how to be set free from doubt and guilt and other emotions that hold us back; and how to live forgiven, free lives in Jesus Christ. We learn how much we are loved—no matter how bad we may think we are.

Although I have been a Christian for over thirty years, it's still exciting to me to think about how joyous one is who knows Christ. As I begin my prayers each morning, I often tear up over the amazing gifts God has given to *me*—a person who absolutely doesn't deserve them. He has heaped happiness on me like dumping a big pile of gaily wrapped gifts over me that have completely covered me up!

If that's the case for me, a person living thousands of years after Christ's presence, how much more the early Christians must have felt that joy. They were right there, present when the exciting news of the gospel was first shared. Yet at least one of them drifted away.

It's a short sentence, easy to miss. But it speaks volumes:

Demas, because he loved this world, has deserted me. (2 Timothy 4:10)

Demas had been with Paul a long time. Although others must have moved on for various reasons, Demas supported Paul even through his imprisonment. But then Demas left. He didn't intentionally, mindfully desert Paul. There wasn't a falling out or a disagreement about Christ's or Paul's teaching. Instead Demas simply drifted away, seduced by the world. And by doing so, he missed his calling: to bring others to Jesus. He missed out on the greatest blessings he could have ever received, and he had already been exposed to them. Imagine knowing the apostles, working side by side with them in the work of saving souls, and rejecting it by walking away.

Pretend for a moment that you are in Demas's shoes. Do you think you would ever look back and miss what you had with Paul? _____

Why or why not? _____

What was Demas's idol? _____

I believe that drifting away from Christ after our declaration of devotion to Him can happen for many reasons, but the root cause is *always* an idol. Remember our definition: anything that repeatedly draws us away from our worship time with the Lord. Something that pulls us, something magnetic that we just can't resist. Something about which we obsess. A false god. An idol.

A verse about this drifting away from the Lord, Hebrews 2:1, has an interesting history. It says, "We must pay much closer attention to what we have heard, so that we do not drift away from it" (NASB). The original translators questioned whether to put in the final two words, "from it," because by including them, we water down the intended message. Take a moment to read that verse now without those last two words, then with them. What do you think? With or without these two words, or those of historical translations (*leak, slip*),[4] I believe it is our soul that will drift, moving away from the Word and therefore the Lord of life.

If we become indifferent to God's message, His Word, His purpose—then we open ourselves to drift. Drifting is wherever, whatever, any old time. It takes no effort; it simply happens. Drifting takes a lifetime full of meaning and purpose and renders it a tragic consequence of the world we live in. Drifting causes us to lose our way. If we don't take care to pay very close attention to our faith, we could even find ourselves shipwrecked.

I knew a classmate in college who had spent his sweet, quiet life in church and wanted to become a teacher—a Bible teacher. He actually didn't mention it the whole first year or so that I knew him. This seemed an impressive goal until you got to know his philosophy a little bit. It was skewed. I tried to be open-minded, but the things he said were so far away from the Bible's text that I became angry every time we talked. It was funny in a way. I liked him until we got into those conversations. Over time, he offered to loan me some books and I began to understand. He wasn't reading biblical materials, but antibiblical. You know those texts I'm talking about, the ones that say there's no way Jesus was any more than a good philosopher, or that He even existed (people "like me" fabricated Jesus, according to my friend). His beliefs shocked me, but they were becoming clearer. As I thought about him teaching young minds these twisted viewpoints, I cringed.

As our friendship developed, he found out I was pretty good with computers, so he asked me to come over to his apartment and fix his. By this time it had been two or three years of two classmates grabbing a quick meal every few weeks. I'd never been to his apartment, nor he to mine. I'm not sure why I continued meeting with him. I guess I hoped I could "save" him.

Upon entering his apartment, I instantly saw at least part of his drift problem. Every surface of the place was littered with cigarette ash and beer cans. When I sat down to work on his computer, I realized another, deeper part of his problem. His computer issues stemmed from the sort of virus that comes in with porn.

"John! You've been looking at porn!" I exclaimed.

"No, I haven't," he replied, looking me steadily in the eyes.

This is what he looks like when he lies, I told myself. But computers don't lie; I had his entire web history right in front of me. Singles ads with his own nude pictures (Nude! Is *that* how we're supposed to do it??), many porn sites, and tons of Trojans (computer style, that is) and viruses. Oh, my. I cleaned up the computer, then I fled.

Like Demas, John had drifted. He may have picked up a magazine and read an anti-Christian article, for example, or it may have been the influence of a professor. Next thing you know, he's questioning the things he once knew to be true. He found lust, sex, porn, and anti-Christianity easier to follow than the truth that is Jesus Christ.

Drifting away from Christ in order to follow a false god, or several, is one of the biggest dangers we face. Worse yet, all seduction is not sexual; the world itself is seductive. Satan knows that drifting is one of the easiest ways to attract us, and he's very good at making it happen. We keep our eyes open for a full-out attack, never realizing it's the small things that will suck us in at first.

To be saved, after all, does not mean safe. We have to watch out because Satan looks for ways he can gain our trust, and he uses those against us. Often it is through a lie that distorts our thinking or confuses our knowledge of the gospel. Once we're a little confused, even for seasoned Christians, it's easy to start drifting away.

Honestly, Christianity requires a lot of work. We must apply effort, diligence, and dedication. We have to show up, whether at church or Bible study or simply in a calm prayer spot alone with God. We have to allow Him to make changes in us, some of which are terribly uncomfortable. Whereas drifting requires nothing at all. It just . . . is.

Drifting away takes place subtly. People who drift don't actively reject faith on some certain premise. They just slowly slip away. Maybe Bible reading becomes mechanical, so they stop studying. They stop worshiping, at least regularly. Or maybe they're in church every week, but the mind wanders. Glance around sometime in your own church for those who aren't really listening or digesting the message. They're just being. Some are making a grocery list or texting. One member sits sipping coffee, looking around her at the others to see who's there. Several look zoned out, as if you could poke them and they'd fall right over on the pew. That's just the beginning . . .

The way God created our hearts is with a void reserved only for Him—so if we don't allow Him there, it becomes empty, but not for long—it is always replaced by something, even if that something ultimately can't fulfill a void meant only for God. Demas was seduced by the world, but what in the world did he love? We aren't told, so we can only guess. But what we can do is be more specific about our own lives. If we see ourselves being seduced by the world, we can put our lives under a microscope and try to figure out exactly what is pulling us in the wrong direction.

Anyway, back to those "other people," those drifters. They may not think of spirituality after a while, or if they do it's confused, mixed in with something they heard on Oprah or read in a novel. At this point, they are suffering from a major compromise of their convictions. I hope you're seeing a big red flag that reads, "Danger," because that's where the drifting person is right now—in danger of falling away.

Does this red flag wave on your behalf, or on that of someone you know? Write their initials here: _____

Pray for that person every day this week.

Day 2: Accountability

$\mathcal{I}$'D LIKE TO MENTION HERE that as Christians, if we see a fellow believer struggling, we have the responsibility to approach the one who is falling away and try to reach him or her on some level. In church we usually refer to this as discipline. Discipline is patterned after God's own holiness, and His desire for the church family to be set apart and holy. Many of us try to avoid this task, because we hate conflict or we think it isn't our place. It is never fun or easy, but as members of the family, disciplining one another is part of our job.

Galatians 6:1 explains why. "Brothers and sisters, if someone is caught in a sin, you who live by the Spirit should restore that person gently. But watch yourselves, or you also may be tempted." Matthew 18:15 explains how. "If your brother or sister sins, go and point out their fault, just between the two of you. If they listen to you, you have won them over."

That's all. Just go talk to them in a loving way. Do not, do not, *do not* under any circumstances go and in abundant detail and with great relish discuss it among others. If you do, you too are sinning and do not need to be the one correcting your brother or sister in Christ.

Approach your friend with a heart of gentleness and meekness, with intent to restore him or her to whom Christ designed that friend to be. This is the way we're taught to reach out to each other. It's an orderly system of all being accountable to one another.

Is there someone you feel is struggling in his or her Christian walk right now? Write his/her initials here: _____

Pray about whether you should discuss the topic with your friend. This is difficult; sometimes you are not the best person for the job. Sometimes, like Jonah, you know you are supposed to go but you are reluctant—even reluctant enough to run away! Much prayer should come before, during and after this event.

Day 3: Idolatry—It's Lethal

USUALLY WHEN SOMEONE DESCRIBES DRIFTING, they use an analogy. Most often it involves water and a dam, with either a bird floating on a piece of wood or two young men out in a boat. The victims for some reason don't realize what's about to happen, and they suddenly fall over the edge of the dam.

I don't have a lot of experience with this analogy, but I do know a kind of drifting that is far more subtle, and maybe more relevant to what we are discussing here. When I was young, my cousin and I loved nothing more than to be the first ones awake when we were at the beach, so we could go out and get in the ocean. We played in water that probably wasn't much above our waists, but we squatted down so we felt like we were in up to our necks. We would play and play until we got hungry, and then we would stand up, look around, and realize we were lost. The current had carried us far from home. It was a momentary situation. We knew which way the current was going and would simply walk back until we found our house. But for a few moments there, we were disoriented.

To me, this is the kind of drift that takes place in the Christian life. You're not doing anything dramatic; you're just absorbed in the world of being you. Then you look up and can't recognize the shoreline. Getting back might not be so easy though, depending on how far you've managed to drift. After all, you can't see the current. On the surface everything looks smooth. And if you get far enough away from land, you don't have a guideline to show you that you're drifting. Without the guideline (Jesus), you care less and less about the drift. But Psalm 119:118 declares it in a rather harsh light:

> "Expose all who drift away from your sayings; their casual idolatry is *lethal*." (MSG, emphasis added)

> There are numerous biblical examples of drift. Probably the earliest example in the Bible was before the flood. The people slowly began to drift away until . . .

> Then the Lord saw that the wickedness of man was great on the earth, and that every intent of the thoughts of his heart was only evil continually. (Genesis 6:5 NASB)

Next we have Israel drifting . . . coming back . . . drifting again . . . until God finally allowed His people to be taken into captivity. Israel was unfaithful, strong-willed, stubborn, and idolatrous on more than one occasion. Some refused to be move from their ungodly paths. They wanted to listen to anybody who would tell them their false gods were acceptable and they would be okay without God or simply with godlessness. Don't you want to just grab those Israelites by their shoulders and shake them? I do. I want to ask them, Dr. Phil style, "What were you *thinking?*"

We're still doing that stuff today. We create functional gods. We go to church and only pretend to pray. We drift. We follow ideas that our Bibles tell us are wrong—and we *know* they are wrong. Ephesians 4:14 tells us that we can easily be "tossed back and forth by the waves, and blown here and there by every wind of teaching and by the cunning and craftiness of people in their deceitful scheming."

There is one special way to know that you yourself are the problem, that you are the one drifting. That's when every godly person in your life is getting on your nerves. Realize then that you must take active steps toward God. It is impossible to drift against the current! The only way to fight it is to swim—hard—against it. I hope you're a good swimmer, because it's incredibly difficult to swim upstream. But if that's what it takes, I'm willing to do it, aren't you?

Do you have a functional god? What is it? _____

What experience or idol in your life has caused you to be "blown here and there by every wind of teaching"?

_____

Has there ever been a time in your life when you have drifted? Describe that experience.

_____

Discuss with the class, if you are able.

Because of sin, sometimes it seems impossible to return to God. The sinner feels dirty and ashamed. One man told me, "If I went to church, I'd be just like those other hypocrites that sit there every week." So he didn't go. He didn't turn his life over or repent. Sadly this man passed away, and as far as I know, never reached out to God. But sin merely is turning *from* God. The true heart *turns around and reaches* for Him. All we have to do is reach our arms out.

Please read Ephesians 1:11, in *The Message* if you have a copy.

Long before we first heard of Christ and got our hopes up, _____

_____

Isn't it wonderful that God had His eye on us first? That means that no matter how far we've drifted, no matter where the crazy currents might have carried us, He is waiting with open arms for us to reach for Him. Just reach out.

After reaching for Him, we are to slowly, carefully build a fortress within ourselves (our heart) where only God and His Word can exist. That's how you get through the busyness and side roads of life. That's how you avoid drifting again.

A relationship with Christ is never stationary. It's either getting better or worse; you're either feeling higher or lower. Often groups are asked to sketch a graph of their walk with Christ. I've never seen one that was a flat line. People experience hills and valleys.

If you don't feel that you're progressing, you are probably digressing. Life in Christ is a living, breathing entity all on its own. Your soul has to be fed and nurtured in the ways that make you feel positive. A spiritual life is the single most important part of you. Make it your priority.

Draw a sketch of your own Christian experience below. Here's an example:

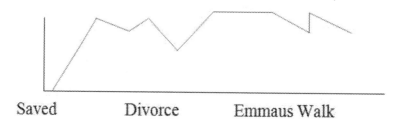

| Saved | Divorce | Emmaus Walk |

Day 4: Casual Christians

WHILE SOME PEOPLE DRIFT, FOR others the gospel isn't worth any regard whatsoever. I'm talking about casual Christians, or careless Christians. Some of these seem never to have changed upon their profession of faith. Many who say they believed in Christ early on become worldly, or casual Christians. Ten or fifteen years ago, the term was *carnal*

Christians. As I consider it, maybe a better descriptive word is *purposeless*. However you want to think of it, it's a worldly lifestyle that doesn't allow God to lead.

People who live this way become sick because their spiritual heart is diseased. But watch out, because the sickness is horribly contagious. Those who have it also have the ability to draw others into their careless, worldly lifestyle. This is one disease we all have to guard against, because it can spread like wildfire.

Casual Christianity is different from drift, though it may start with drifting. Eventually it's much more than that. It is rebellious. It is driven by a false doctrine with an empty philosophy. It is sensual, indulgent, and sinful.

A casual Christian is hard-hearted. He generally quotes Scripture incorrectly, if at all. He enjoys only those parts of Scripture that are relevant to his own distorted view of life. He also may church hop, because as he finds himself less influential in one church, he'll simply move on to destroy the next.

If you think my words are harsh, you're right. I mean to be. There is no room in the church for casual Christians, purposeless Christians—people who not only let Satan in but invite him in, tell him what time to come, hold the door open, and give him the best seat.

The church is meant to have one sound doctrine. Casual Christians exploit it and mislead others along the way.

Please read Titus 1:16.

The text describes casual Christians this way: _____

How do these people fail to grow spiritually after they have experienced the wonderful love of Jesus? Here's my guess: church attendance may be part of their lives, but I suspect they are passive participants. They don't have any intention of thinking about what happened in church after they leave. They have no plans to apply the concepts they've learned in church to their daily lives. Like Demas, they are seduced by the world.

Perhaps these are the people James was thinking of when he wrote:

> "Don't fool yourself into thinking that you are a listener when you are anything but, letting the Word go in one ear and out the other. Act on what you hear! Those who hear and don't act are like those who glance in the mirror, walk away, and 2 minutes later have no idea who they are, what they look like." (James 1:22 –24 MSG)

It is true that God's mercy and grace can cover all sins, including those committed by casual Christians. But within the depths of that mercy, we cannot allow ourselves to become arrogant by thinking we can continually do whatever we want, carelessly unrepentant, and God will keep forgiving us. He only forgives us when we come back to Him, when our heart is once again longing for His love.

When believers don't listen to God, they listen to others: friends, TV, news articles, the Internet. These become their main influences. A friend is only as good as his heart is, and we can assume that a casual Christian usually befriends other purposeless Christians. If his friends were more sincere, they would encourage him to listen to God—which is what he doesn't want to do. And don't even get me started on media influence! Let's just say it usually has little to do with Christianity.

Let's take a look at Michael, a forty-something man who can quote the Bible, as they say, backward and forward. He often volunteers to work at church functions and practices good stewardship. But get to know him a little bit and you'll be shocked. "Those church people," he says. "You can't trust 'em as far as you can throw 'em."

What? Then what's his motivation to be around them?

He's been married since he was nineteen, but when Michael speaks to his wife on the phone you have to wonder how she's put up with him. "What!?" he answers gruffly, while hanging out with friends. "I'm trying to do business here. I'll talk to you later."

Not only does he lie to his wife but his family says that if he's talking, he's lying. So the next time you hear him quote the Bible in Sunday school, you aren't nearly as impressed as you were before.

It's hard to explain how this man can know the Word, yet not carry it in his heart. Somewhere along the way he became deceived—and has stayed that way.

Do you think Michael has a false or functional god? _____

What is it? _____

LeAnn is a lot like Michael. She's very involved in her church, but a friend came to me to discuss how she should handle a situation with LeAnn. My friend wanted to do the right thing. During the discussion I realized who we were talking about. I have to say I was stunned.

It seems LeAnn went to a local business without an appointment, and when told she would have to make one or wait, she became a prima donna, screaming at the receptionist as she left, "I will never come here again!" The receptionist was young, so she didn't have much experience with this sort of thing, and she had no authority to make changes without the owner's permission. LeAnn wanted her to anyway. My friend was nervous about confronting LeAnn and wanted to do it via an anonymous email.

What do you think my advice should have been?

_____

How would you have handled the situation?

_____

Believers who aren't listening to God are usually not actively in the Scripture, and when we don't know Scripture, we can become deceived, drifting into sin without meaning to. That's what is so dangerous about the casual nature of this lukewarm Christian.

> Jesus said, "Put your mind on your life with God. The way to life—to God!—is vigorous and requires your total attention." (Luke 13:24 MSG)

If you keep your mind as Jesus tells us to, the lukewarm, carnal Christian will not be able to seduce you into following him or her. Whether the seduction is literal or figurative, we must be on guard against these people. They're all around.

Casual Christians often cajole or bully their way into leadership positions. Sometimes we select them because they have strong personalities, which we perceive as positive leadership style. No matter what the excuse for choosing them, they are the last people we as Christians should want in a guidance role, whether in our church or merely on the board of some volunteer organization. By observing the behavior of a person over time, it becomes easy to identify a casual Christian. He or she is the one with the critical spirit, who almost immediately rejects new or different ideas without really hearing them out. That rejection also carries over to people, especially those whom they sense might be a threat to their role.

Often casual Christians become hateful and abuse their position of power once they achieve it. They may use mean tactics to sway others to their opinions. They may gather their own groupies privately who will become their yes-men in public. If you walk into a meeting and realize that four or five other members have been discussing the topic privately and already come to a somewhat convoluted conclusion, you are probably looking at casual Christians.

These people are completely unacceptable to be leaders of other Christians, whether in church or outside it. I feel so strongly about this because I often discern people like this who are leading or hold power positions as detrimental to the church. They will ultimately leave a path of destruction behind them, whether individuals or entire groups. They have the ability to destroy the whole church. I've seen it happen, and I suspect you have as well.

Part of our job as true Christians is to guard against this by selecting leaders who hold themselves to a higher standard. It is up to us to be sure that those who lead do so in a kind, merciful, and loving way. If love is not part of his or her leadership style, move on. Don't be swayed by the popularity contests or the insistence of his or her friends. We are commanded to love and act as one in the church—let this be your guide.

Worse yet, be careful that casual Christians are never the teachers of young children, whose minds they have such power to sway. Something stated incorrectly by a teacher can remain in a child's mind for years, and truly hamper that young one's Christian walk.

The false doctrine of a casual Christian may not be on purpose; that person may not be in the Word enough to realize her ideas have flaws. Or perhaps she has never been in the Bible at all. A casual Christian doesn't hold anything in her heart but simply goes through the motions. Remember what happens with that God-void in our heart? If we don't fill it with God, something else moves in.

A casual Christian's attitude is complacent, believing any lifestyle is acceptable to God. He doesn't follow the rules, and the Word is not written on his heart. Any false doctrine spoken by such a person has the potential to lead others astray. That is not what we want in our church.

The book of Jude is only a page and a half in my Bible. It's a letter that Jude, the brother of James, wrote begging the people to fight against some deceptive individuals who had infiltrated the church. "Fight with everything you have in you for this faith entrusted to us as a gift to guard and cherish," he implores them (Jude 4 MSG).

Jude realized that these false teachers were telling the congregation that the grace of God gave them license to do anything. This caused confusion within the church, and the church became divided. Jude said we absolutely must stand on the Word of God. It is not unusual for a group of casual Christians to infiltrate the church's Interior Department even today.

Jude wrote that two thousand years ago, but it is still the solution to the presence of casual Christians. That's God's perfection at work. We have to guard and cherish our gift if we want to keep it.

This week, read Jude's letter.

Day 5: Opening Our Hearts for Scrutiny

As TIME GOES ON, A casual Christian doesn't just forget or ignore the Word. He may begin to outright reject biblical passages that might condemn him for his choices. The story is told that Thomas Jefferson did just that. He used scissors to cut up his Bible and put back together only the parts he wanted. Jefferson considered himself a Christian, yet rejected (among other things) the idea of the Trinity.

This is a point we really need to pay attention to. If we were dogs, this is when we would sit up tall and perk up our ears. If we reject any word of Scripture, it is time for a deep, long, heart check. Because probably whatever we reject is addressing *our very own behavior.*

That's why we must seek what is real and what is truth, with everything in us. By doing so we can let God do the painful rearranging He must do inside our hearts. If we allow it, He can get to every part of us—there is nothing we hold back or block off from His scrutiny. That way we are able to grow and bear fruit, not drift or become casual about our faith. We can't be passive if God is helping us grow.

Negative decisions we make and sinful choices will mark our lives forever. We are changed in a way that leaves us permanently scarred, and we almost always hurt those around us during those seasons. But by opening our hearts and letting God reach every part of us, even those areas we believe are dark and secret, we can live a beautiful and joyous life. We will never be the ones who are casual or drifting.

I've joined together drifting and casual Christianity because it is so easy to slide from one into the other. In many ways, they are the same. So our questions for this week address both:

Read 1 John 2:16. Depending on which version you read, your answers will be different. List the nouns you see: ⎯⎯⎯⎯⎯⎯⎯⎯⎯⎯⎯⎯⎯⎯

Can you think of anything you lust, boast, or crave after? Write it here: ⎯⎯⎯⎯⎯⎯

⎯⎯⎯⎯⎯⎯⎯⎯⎯⎯⎯⎯⎯⎯⎯⎯⎯⎯⎯⎯⎯⎯⎯⎯⎯⎯⎯⎯⎯⎯⎯⎯⎯⎯⎯⎯⎯⎯

Read 2 Peter 1:5–8. What are we told to do that will help us to avoid becoming a drifting, purposeless Christian?

⎯⎯⎯⎯⎯⎯⎯⎯⎯⎯⎯⎯⎯⎯⎯⎯⎯⎯⎯⎯⎯⎯⎯⎯⎯⎯⎯⎯⎯⎯⎯⎯⎯⎯⎯⎯⎯⎯

How can you apply that this week to your own life?

_____

_____

Hebrews 2:1 says, "It's crucial that we keep a firm grip on what we've heard so that we don't drift off" (MSG). If you realize you are in danger of drifting, walk toward God with sorrow for the drift, but with a renewed commitment and submission. Spiritual drifting is not an overnight activity, so it won't be a one-day trip back either. It must be done with deliberate steps. If this is you, name some of the concrete steps you will take today:

1.

2.

3.

Dear Lord, I have come to You with a willing and open heart. Please take all of it, 100 percent. Help me to see what's happening if I ever begin to drift, and lead me back to Your straight paths. Amen.

WEEK 3

A Week without My Little Gods

"Human life is a struggle, isn't it? It's a life sentence to hard labor."
—Job 7:1 (MSG)

THE GOD-SHAPED VOID THAT LIVES inside each of our hearts makes us all seekers. We are all looking for something. We desire a fulfillment that we are so increasingly aware we lack. We want the benefits of God—peace, joy, and love. We want to go to heaven. In fact, 85 percent of Americans believe they are going to heaven.

Yet people often don't want to seek out God Himself—won't or can't reach out for the relationship we must have if we want all those fringe benefits. You do. That's why you are in this study. In order to get that right relationship, you have realized you have to sacrifice. Not because we have to suffer to know God, but because He knows that after you have experienced suffering, you will realize even more peace, love, and joy in your life.

Read Romans 5:1–2.

How did we receive grace? _____

How did we find peace with God? _____

Do you feel this peace now? _____

If not, do you know why? _____

Discuss this with your group, if you are able.

Romans 5:2 tells us that we have personal access to the Lord of the universe. Take hold of that gift and use it for all it is worth! You can only gain true peace, joy, and hope through that relationship with God. I don't know about you, but I'm willing to do whatever it takes to create and maintain that relationship.

I have talked to people who have contemplated suicide, and they tell me that they become suicidal when there is no hope.

Write Romans 5:5 here:

_____

_____

Why is this hope different from the world's hope? _____

_____

So we have peace, hope, and love because of our Savior. This week we're going to work hard at clearing out the clutter between us and our right relationship with Him. It will be challenging. We've touched on our functional gods in the first two weeks.

Please recall here what yours are:

_____

Day 1: Self-Importance

IN AMERICA WE CONSIDER OURSELVES indomitable. I saw a headline just this morning: "Obama Says America Is Still a Powerhouse." What does that mean, other than we are going to crush the competition, pushing anyone aside that stands in our way? And what does a domination mentality say about our Christianity?

We have more freedom than any other country in the world, and we use that freedom to abuse drugs, alcohol, pornography, sex, and violence. That is not freedom at all. We are creating bondage. By allowing these things into our minds, we break not only the country's law but God's law. We create idols.

Many Christians seem to consider our freedom a license to do whatever they want. Breaking God's law does not have any repercussions, they think. Or perhaps they believe that since they said a prayer to accept Jesus Christ as Savior, they're now covered and can sin without consequence. This is wrong thinking. God's blessing does not give us the right to covet the things the world believes create quality of life.

Even the church is susceptible to this mentality. I can't name any church that does not encourage its members to covet what the world believes is important. Yet Jesus died on the cross to save us from the penalty of sin. He did not do this so we could indulge in our own lust and desire. He did not sacrifice Himself so we could live selfishly. True freedom is when we surrender our lives to Jesus Christ and remove the bondage of sin we create through idols.

I believe that our current culture has taught us much of our self-centeredness. We're full of self-concern, self-importance, ego, and busyness. Yes, even busyness qualifies as self-centeredness, for what is it, really, other than a refusal to let go of things that might be less important?

"I'm the only one who can lead this group," one board member told me. In reality, anyone on that board could have led. When the ego is this large, it is easy for the group or company or anything else that person touches to suffer. What is her idol? Self.

Self as an idol is the hardest to recognize and the hardest to control. Are you really going to suddenly see it and say, "I've had myself on the pedestal all this time"? Even when one does see it, self is a pervasive little god; it jumps up on the pedestal again and again.

Here's the secret about self as an idol. We're taught to do it. From an early age, we are taught to love ourselves, promote ourselves, and guard ourselves at all costs. We are taught to compete, to win. Winning is good; losing, or simply not competing, is not acceptable.

We're promoting this selfishness in our children as well. We want them to have:

» self-sufficiency

» self-esteem

» self-confidence

We treat our children like functional little gods. Yet an exaggerated sense of self-importance leads young people to create their own rules. They don't care who they step on in their climb to the top. They don't follow the mandates set out by society or convention. They don't care who they hurt. Their idol is "me." Or better, "me-me-me."

All sorts of studies try to explain the rash of young narcissists we've created. I've read studies that blame talk radio, Facebook, Twitter, and plain old bad parenting for this phenomenon. But when you get right down to it, the egocentric young person holds self as his or her idol. And we, the older generation, have taught them exactly how to do it.

Worshiping the Gift but Not the Giver

Another way idols can be created is when a person has worked diligently to receive blessings—gifts—from God. His relationship with God begins to suffer. That's because when he receives these blessings, he often sees them as achievements and forgets about God and His presence. As an example, let's consider John, who worked hard all his life in the corporate world and received many accolades and several promotions. Over the years he also became a strong leader in his church. Then John was made vice president of his company.

John no longer thanks God for this blessing he has received. Privately he believes the promotion was rightfully his, and that he is the one who sacrificed over the years, devoting his time and efforts for the gains he's made. He planned his life around this company for over thirty years, and look where it has brought him. John has become full of self-importance. He feels entirely self-sufficient.

At the same time, John is seen around the church less and less. He has relinquished some of his leadership roles. "Just don't have the time," he explains.

Of course everyone respects his new position and the stress it probably has put on him, so no one says what they are thinking. John has lost sight of the Giver and has put his interests only in the gifts. His relationship with God has already suffered, and will suffer more if he continues on this path. In fact, sometimes God has to take away the blessings to bring the sinner's attention back to Himself.

This reminds us of the parable in Luke 12, when the rich man had abundant grain but didn't think to thank God for the blessing. He was going to store the grain and retire for the rest of his life. Jesus took the story as an opportunity to warn the people, "Be on your guard against every form of greed; for not even when one has an abundance does his life consist of his possessions" (v. 15 NASB).

In fact, our life *never* consists of our possessions. Unfortunately, the more we have, the more we lose sight of that fact. Paul, a second-generation Pharisee, went from having everything to losing everything to going to prison for his beliefs. That's when he wrote:

> I know what it is to be in need, and I know what it is to have plenty. I have learned the secret of being content in any and every situation, whether well fed or hungry, whether living in plenty or in want. I can do all this through him who gives me strength. (Philippians 4:12–13)

Can you say that you are content in each and every situation? _____

Why or why not? _____

_____

Would you have felt as content as Paul did if you were imprisoned?_____

_____

In Genesis 4, Cain pouted because Abel's sacrifice to God was more pleasing than his. Cain merely brought "some" of the delicious produce he grew. Abel, on the other hand, presented to God his choicest portions from the firstborn of his flocks. God reminded Cain, "Sin is crouching at your door; it desires to have you, but you must rule over it" (v. 7).

It appears Cain held himself in great esteem. He was proud, too proud to let God have the best of his fruits. When we refuse to take a warning like the above—*sin is crouching at your door*—we open the way for sin to indeed rule over us. Sin got ahold of Cain, and he murdered his brother rather than listen to what God was telling him.

Even today, like Cain, we sometimes don't listen to a clear warning from God. When we refuse to acknowledge that idols do happen in today's society—in our own lives—we are also unwilling to learn how to guard against them. By ignoring the truth, we are more likely to become the victim of idol worship.

Day 2: I'm Too Busy!

WE ALL CONSIDER OURSELVES BUSY—AND we are. Everyone rushes from one activity to the next. No wonder we have little time to spend with God. I have one friend

I'm awed by because I can't understand how she manages to do so much. She participates in every church activity, Bible studies, social groups, and entertains regularly, all while keeping a perfect house and staying in touch with all her friends.

For others of us though, so much busyness would not result in fruitfulness. That's one area where the Holy Spirit can help us decide whether to say yes or no. God doesn't mean for us to pursue every opportunity, but only the ones that will move us forward in our relationship and walk with Him.

When I started writing this book, I found myself covered with busyness. *Excuses*, I thought, *excuses for not writing*. I made a list of the things I would say yes to (meaning that everything else had to get a no). My yes list included God, church, writing, friends, and family; and groups I'm already in, but no new groups. By default my many hobbies (beading, planted aquariums, pets) had to fall in line behind the yes group, and some went on hold for a while. Obviously I have to brush and feed the dog, but not start making a new necklace, for example. Everything that was not a yes became a no. I had to carefully guard my work and my time.

This also meant unplugging the telephone and sometimes the Internet. It meant I could go to the movies with my husband and our friends occasionally—something we both need, as we both work from home—but I couldn't chat idly on the phone for an hour every day. I simply didn't have that kind of time.

I could have let things continue as they were, full of scattered thoughts and precious little writing time. I would have then been full of self-importance: "I'm writing a book," I could say, but it wouldn't really be true, would it? The ego would exist as an idol, and the book would remain unwritten.

James Packer said, "In the matter of life's basic loyalty, temptation is a many-headed monster."[5]

If you are short on time, make a list of the things you need to say yes to.

_____

_____

_____

_____

What things will you say no to?

_____

_____

_____

_____

Day 3: Identifying your Idol/Habit

I WENT ON ONE OF THOSE celebrity diets once. My daughter wanted to lose a little weight, and I agreed to do it with her. The first thing we had to do was cut out all carbohydrates—bread, potatoes, and sweets. The book warned us that our bodies would have a reaction if we were "addicted" to carbs. Since I didn't consider myself addicted to anything, I wasn't worried.

Boy, was I in for a surprise. My brain had gotten used to the biochemicals I received from the large amount of bread I ate. Just like a heroin addict, I craved bread. I felt jittery and agitated without it. This went on for a couple of weeks, but it was a great wake-up call. Ever since, I've watched the amount of bread I eat because I don't want to become addicted again.

Just like my carb addiction, many of us are "addicted" to our computers, smart phones, Kindles, iPads, TVs, and other gadgets. I say addicted because they take the place of everything I/we *should* be doing. We feel lost without them, we suffer withdrawal. So this week, I'm going to ask you to detox yourself from the functional god we mentioned earlier. It might be your computer or a favorite gadget. For some it will be a television show or two, rather than an object. Or it may be gaming.

Some of you will say that you're not a gadget addict, but you love clothes, fashion, shoes, or makeup. You may love your house, or telling about your extravagant vacations. It could be that you slightly fudge on your medication, taking more than the prescribed dose. Or maybe you know you're abusing a substance—drugs, alcohol, caffeine. Maybe it's sex. Whatever it is, I'm asking you to give up the one thing that drives most of your time and thought for just one week. Remember, we're making the sacrifice so that we have more time to spend with God—in prayer, in the Bible, and simply sitting and listening for His perfect guidance.

If your addiction is more serious than these we discuss rather lightheartedly, I urge you to get help for it. This week, pick up the phone and find where you're going to get that help. It may be an addiction treatment center, your physician, or your church counselor. You may need to check into a full-time treatment facility. Whatever your need is, please know that the rest of your group is fully behind you as you face the demon—and win.

The main thing I absolutely can't live without is: _____

I know this is scary. I've done it myself. For a long time, early in my writing career, I guess you could say I was addicted to email. It's so easy when your work involves sitting in front of a computer to check your email a thousand times, especially when you live and work alone. I was wasting many hours on email instead of writing. It kept me from meeting my writing goals.

I have a time log, a chart that simply lists the day in fifteen-minute increments, from the time I get up to the time I go to bed. When I'm not meeting goals, I make myself fill in what I was doing on that chart. It makes you very honest—two hours in email means you have to write it down eight times! So I used my chart and saw how much I was in my email. *Yuk.*

Here are the steps I took to solve my email addiction:

1. I chose two times to look in my e-mail each day. I have to look at it, because editors might give me responses to something I've written, and I need to get back to them. So completely avoiding it was not an option. Instead I decided to check email at 9 a.m. and 4 p.m. Those two times gave me enough time to respond to people in the same business day, and allowed me to do all my writing in between or afterward.

2. I wrote to all the friends who send several forwards every day, and asked them to take me off their email list. This did not make me popular. Several friends were quite angry. This is one case where self is not an idol. Instead it's self-preservation, especially for a then-single, full-time writer.

3. I unsubscribed from everything—every single newsletter. If I want to go shopping, I know how to find them; I don't need an email reminder. If I want a coupon, there's usually one on the Internet.

It wasn't perfect, because for the first three weeks, I found myself checking email at the wrong time. But the email wasn't so interesting, what with rejecting all my friends and retail outlets. As soon as I realized what I was doing, I closed it. Occasionally I pulled the Internet cord out of the computer for the day so I *couldn't* get to email. If I idly clicked on email, I would get a message that I wasn't connected, which reminded me why. Eventually the schedule all fell into place.

One of the most important things we must realize is that we alone have no power against our idols. I remember one time I was in a meeting with a counselor at an addiction center. She tried to explain this lack of power to me. "Have you ever dieted?" she asked. Now, this was funny to me because she was about 100 pounds overweight. It was also when I weighed about 130 pounds total. Why should I diet?

"No," I answered.

"Oh, well, it's like if there is a piece of cake sitting here," indicating her desk, "and you know you aren't supposed to eat it. But it's there tempting you, and you can't help it. You just have to eat the cake."

This told me nothing. I ate so much that it was a joke among friends. I had no concept of rejecting the cake, so her analogy didn't work for me.

Now that I've gotten overweight and fought it out, I can completely relate to the cake analogy. In fact, now one of my own battles is with peanut butter. Refusing to eat it is a daily fight, especially after 7 p.m. (my own cutoff time for eating). I sit and think, *I will not eat peanut butter, I will not eat peanut butter.* The more I think, the more I imagine that jar in front of me. Even if I manage not to eat it while I'm up, I'll sometimes wake up in the night believing that I'm hungry, and perhaps eat some then.

That's an idol for you. It takes over. It reaches out and grabs your mind so that you seem unable to think of anything else. It tells you that you *must have it,* that you *can't wait until tomorrow or even another moment.*

While you're detoxing from your favorite time-stealer, watch for uncharacteristic behavior. When we take a week away from something we love, strange things happen. You can expect to feel disconnected, confused, or lost at times. It would be great to keep a journal of your feelings this week and share them with the rest of the group next week.

Does giving up your favorite thing make you feel like the Lone Ranger? If it does, consider making a commitment together as a group. You can practice fighting the craving together, and phone each other when you're feeling weak. Girls do this after a breakup, to keep from calling the ex-boyfriend. Paul mentioned something similar in Romans 1:11–12,

"I long to see you so that I may impart to you some spiritual gift to make you strong—that is, that you and I may be mutually encouraged by each other's faith."

Sometimes rather than drawing closer to God, people substitute a new functional god to take the place of the old one. So if you find yourself doing something that's entirely uncharacteristic, it would be a good time to stop what you are doing and pray. Especially if your idol is drugs, alcohol, or sexual in nature, you will need to be extradiligent in moving out the idol and making sure it is truly God that you move into its place.

Please read Ephesians 6:10–18. Which part of the armor of God do you relate to most in your own battle? _____

Prayer is mentioned in verse 18 but not listed as a specific weapon. That's because the key to consistent victory is consistent prayer. It gives us clear guidance and prevents or clears up confusion. It can help us avoid making costly errors. Prayer gives us peace and confidence to move forward and increases our ability to see beyond the surface to the spiritual implications of a situation.

Remember when David battled Goliath? If it's been a while, please read 1 Samuel 17. The Philistines and the Israelites were somewhat at an impasse. Battle lines had been drawn, and the giant Goliath kept coming from the Philistine side to taunt Israel. No one would fight against him.

David was Jesse's youngest son and little more than a boy. He was out herding sheep when his father sent him to take his brothers some food in the warrior camp. David offered to go fight Goliath. He told the giant, "You come against me with sword and spear and javelin, but I come against you in the name of the Lord Almighty, the God of the armies of Israel, whom you have defied" (v. 45), then he killed him with a mere slingshot.

It was not when David aimed the stone at the giant that he won the battle. He won because of his relationship with God. That is how we win or lose, by the way we walk beside our Lord. Prayer gives you a stronger stand against evil than any other influence you can name. Prayer is keeping your mind constantly open to His leadership, so that your constant communion with Him makes you *know* He loves you, beyond the shadow of a doubt.

The biggest battle we have is in our minds, which is where the enemy likes to attack us the most. It could happen this week, while we're trying to get rid of these functional gods. One of his favorite methods of attack is to injure our belief in our own salvation. By yanking the rug out from under our feet, he causes us to question that assurance.

Don't allow it. Never let that doubt creep in. The wonderful reality is that the truth belongs to every follower of Christ. When you put on His armor, you are safe. His life surrounds you. You are his friend! So "put on Christ"—He is your victory.

Day 4: Watch What you Watch

WHEN WE WATCH TELEVISION OR movies, we can hardly do so without encountering sex, cursing, and violence. Do we then become susceptible to those sins? Do we find them more acceptable because we're exposed to them nightly or weekly? In other words—where do we stand as Christians on the topic of viewing sin?

Write your thoughts here: _____

Media has a tremendous influence on all of us, because promoting evil (sin) is done by presenting it in an appealing way. Let's look at one of the biggest modern-day trends on television: the reality show. On many reality shows, gossip—remember, it's a sin equal to murder in God's eyes—is regularly a part of what goes on. Even if the characters aren't gossiping with each other, they gossip to the camera about each other.

But we know these shows aren't real, they're staged. So why does it matter whether we watch them? The answer is that these type of shows use sin to entertain viewers. And any use of sin, however innocuous it seems, can lead us down the path of drift, because it breaks down our invisible barriers of integrity.

Writer C. J. Mahaney talks of watching television proactively.[6] Sin is worthless. So grab the remote and change the channel. Have you ever done this? Do you have the guts to do it?

Does this mean we can't watch any TV at all? What about movies?

You may feel that television and even movie watching takes place behind closed doors. We don't have to discuss it, so we feel as if we aren't accountable. We need deeper discernment though, and higher standards if we are to avoid loving the world. And sometimes, in order to bring healing, we need to take a break from certain shows or types of shows and/or movies.

I struggled with writing this section about the media because I'm certainly not the media police. I did spend most of my life, by choice, not watching television. I didn't even let my children watch *Sesame Street*! I guess this alone makes me an oddity. I homeschooled them, and during that time we did not watch television either. When I moved to Tennessee, we no longer homeschooled but I still didn't have a television in the living room, preferring to spend what little time we had together talking to each other.

That's the first thing children from other families noticed when they walked into our house.

"Where's the TV?" they asked in amazement.

What was amazing to me was that they noticed so quickly!

Now that I'm older and the kids are gone, I watch more television. So I have a reverse situation from most people, and possibly a greater discernment for how TV affects us. It often breaks my heart. I suspect that the general American population doesn't realize how strongly advertising sways their opinions, or how the constant barrage of violence and foul language makes them nearly immune to it in real life, simply because of their constant exposure to it. Or how the noise can block a still, small voice.

But at any rate, I'm not here to tell you to put the TV in the closet, and that's not what my book is about. Choosing exposure to newspapers, books, magazines, television, and the Internet is a personal choice. It's between you and your God, and not for any one writer to dictate. Look at this verse from *The Message*.

> So, friends, we can now—without hesitation—walk right up to God, into "the Holy Place." (Hebrews 10:19 MSG)

Take a walk right up to Him, if you haven't already, and have a discussion about your choice of media and what's right for you. If it's appropriate, give up one of those for the week.

Talking the Talk

A lot of women love to talk on the phone. And when we do, it is rare that we can do it without gossiping. Gossip is one of our biggest downfalls. I love James because his writing makes many things crystal clear, including gossip:

> Those who consider themselves religious and yet do not keep a tight rein on their tongues deceive themselves, and their religion is worthless. (James 1:26)

Worthless!

Please write your thoughts about this verse here.

_____

Gossip is defined as "idle talk or rumor about the personal or private affairs of others."[7] It's a close relative of slander, and God's Word lumps this together with murder and other sins. As a Christian, you probably don't go around stealing things or committing murder—but do you pass on rumors about others? Do you engage in idle talk or bad-mouthing? Look in your Bible and find out which one is the worst sin: murder or gossip? (*Hint*: read Romans 1:28–32.)

Write your thoughts about this here:

_____

The apostle Paul said that one was just as bad as the other! Unfortunately most of us don't see gossip as a sin. It runs rampant in the church, which usually has its own full set of busybodies, and they can cause irreparable harm to the body of Christ. I could tell you stories . . . Oh, guess not.

Many people have been completely drained of their own desire to live for God through others' mean, vicious accusations and rumors. Even leaders have been affected. Gossip can create strife and cause division within the church. It is nothing less than verbal assassination.

My husband and I had a store together. His side was an antiques business, and mine was musical instruments. When we closed our store in 2011, we did so out of the mutual desire to pursue our second jobs; Mickey's is doing antique appraisals, and mine was writing this book. But someone started some gossip that we were having financial troubles. We were surprised, and a little hurt considering the source—someone we thought was a friend. It made us uneasy around everyone from our circle of friends, and a bit defensive. We felt as if we could only discuss our success, and kept the struggles of the change from them. One person's words caused us to take a giant step back from the friends we knew.

Gossip is wicked, a sign of sickness in one's spiritual heart. The mouth is used as a weapon with which we assist Satan in his attempt to "steal and kill and destroy" (John 10:10). Gossip is a deadly disease that can spread like wildfire through a group of friends or an entire church. You might wonder, if it's so bad, how can it spread so easily? The answer is that it is so subtle—and so enticing. Whenever we hear of a secret, we want to be in on it. So we get lured into the trap by listening.

Sometimes gossip is disguised as concern. If a discussion seems entirely negative and sensational rather than trying to solve a problem, it's probably just gossip. You might even agree, sort of, and next thing you know, the gossip has stirred up some dissension that includes *your* name.

Many people are way more interested in stirring than solving.

Is gossip your little god?

The Bible tells us exactly what to do about gossip:

» Avoid associating with people who gossip. "A gossip betrays a confidence; so avoid anyone who talks too much" (Proverbs 20:19).

» Know that God holds you accountable for your words. "But I tell you that everyone will have to give account on the Day of Judgment for every empty word they have spoken. For by your words you will be acquitted, and by your words you will be condemned" (Matthew 12:36–37).

» Participating in gossip shows that you aren't in a right relationship with God. "They have become filled with every kind of wickedness, evil, greed and depravity. . . . They are gossips, slanderers, God-haters, insolent, arrogant and boastful" (Romans 1: 29–30).

» If your friend begins bad-mouthing someone else, stop him or her immediately— refuse to be a part of the sin. "If a person is involved in some serious sins, you don't want to become an unwitting accomplice. In any event, keep a close check on yourself" (1 Timothy 5:22 MSG).

Romans 8:6 reminds us, "For to set the mind on the flesh is death, but to set the mind on the Spirit is life and peace" (ESV).

Day 5: Signs and Tests

" *I* WAS SURE YOU WOULD."

Two women I'd just met were visiting at my house talking about an upcoming wedding. I was to play the music on my violin. Something told me they were not Christians, but they asked for some "churchy-type music" (their words) to be intermingled with the other tunes they had chosen for the prewedding session. I nodded my head and said I knew plenty of appropriate songs, and that is when the comment was made. It wasn't quite a snide remark, but there was a certain tone to it. No matter; I shrugged it off, as I was perfectly capable of providing what they wanted.

I couldn't wait for them to leave though, so I could see what they saw. As soon as they did, I ran to the loveseat they'd sat on and sat down myself. Looking around, I saw:

» an antique painting of Joseph, Mary, and Jesus

» my Bible, current Bible study book, and pens and highlighters on the coffee table

» several hymnals on the bookcase (I have a thing for old ones)

» two shelves of Christian books, also on the bookcase

» a note card with a Bible memory verse written on it on the mantel

Oh. I guess it was pretty evident. Up until then, I hadn't thought much about what my home said about my faith. I only thought it was what you did and said that counted. But since then I've made sure that even if someone walks into my home and doesn't know me, even if they don't hear it, they can see who I am and what I stand for.

Can your guests see or hear that faith is present? _____ ?

Why or why not?_____

Testing Your Functional Gods

By now you have a pretty good idea of what your little gods are. Use these questions to help you decide just how "godly" they are to you.

1. Which ones help you walk with Christ?

2. Which ones honor God?

3. Are they lesser evils? _____ Compared to what?_____

4. Is your priority of life your relationship with God?

5. Do you immediately go to Him when life gives you trials or difficulty?

6. Do you have a servant spirit?

7. What god or idol are you giving up for the next week? _____

8. How do you plan to go about keeping it away? (Example: visual reminders, family help, support from this group, etc.) _____

9. You may not be completely giving something up. Many mature Christians find they need to make small adjustments instead. One lady gave up one day a week of golfing to spend more time with her husband. Another realized she needed to connect more with people and is doing so by writing them cards. If God is directing you to make an adjustment, what is it? _____

10. What are the steps you will take to complete the change? _____

_____

Remember, all that you are and all that you have is a gift from God. Show the world this week that your heart belongs exclusively to Him.

Dear Lord, all that I am and all that I have are Yours. Help me to belong only to You, and to let go of the extraneous parts of life that drive me in the wrong direction. Strengthen me during this time of change. Amen.

A Week with the (Di)Vine

See what great love the Father has lavished on us, that
we should be called children of God!
—1 John 3:1

OW WAS YOUR WEEK WITHOUT a functional god? Was it difficult? Strange? Easier than you expected?

Hopefully, each member of the group found it encouraging to realize this is movement *in the direction of the Savior's loving arms.* Making a sacrifice in Jesus' name never goes unnoticed. Folks—we are on the right path.

Day 1: Feel the Love

THOUGHT THAT AFTER A STRANGE and difficult week of "giving up" something, perhaps we would enjoy spending a week with our Savior. I hope you will immerse yourself in Him this week, fill yourself with His Spirit and His love. Lean back in His arms and let yourself feel loved. If you have a hard time feeling that love, if your spirit blocks it for some reason, ask the Holy Spirit to guide you to Scriptures that will help you feel the love. Claim the following:

> "He who has My commandments and keeps them is the one who loves Me; and he who loves Me will be loved by My Father, and *I will love him and will disclose Myself to him.*" (John 14:21 NASB, emphasis added)

Read 1 John 3 and/or Psalm 45 to help you truly feel the endless love the Lord has for you.

While working on this week's writing, I've been doing a Precepts study by Kay Arthur called *Count It All Joy.* We have read Philippians, chapter 1, written by Paul while he was in prison. I wanted to share one of my observations with you. Here is what I wrote about Paul in the margin: "He is so happy, he sees the good in the circumstances. (Do we give thanks when it happens to us?)"

Paul counted everything joy, even his imprisonment. He was so focused on sharing the gospel that it truly did not matter to him where he was or how much stuff he owned. He simply wanted to share the news of Christ Jesus. I can't imagine sitting in a cold, dark, and probably damp jail cell feeling overjoyed and singing worship songs. But that's what Paul did. Are you feeling down at this moment? Do you often feel overwhelmed? My husband, Mickey, and I are in the middle of cleaning out our house to sell right now. I have said "overwhelmed" so often that I have shortened the word. Now I'm just "whelmed." Every single night—whelmed. That's why it is 1:07 a.m. and I'm writing. That's why last night I was still up at 3 a.m. If that is similar to where you are, you may find it difficult to share Paul's joy.

It is important for all of us to realize that a personal prison can be a lot of things besides a jail cell. You may be so overcome with the sheer stress of life you aren't sure you can bear it. Your body may have started rebelling with insomnia, nervousness, or gastric problems. You might be filled with brokenness or victim-itis or darkness, but God still loves you. If God has begun the work of salvation in you—which we know He did—He did so because He was drawing you to Himself. He wants you in his family! Therefore He will see the work in you through to completion. Maybe you can't see the way out of your prison at this moment, *but He can.*

The first part of John 15:16 says, "You did not choose me, but I chose you and appointed you."

What a delightful thought, that our Lord chose us personally! If you have nothing else to be joyful for today, you have that. Grab that joy and hold on to it, savor it, and send it back to Him with your thankful heart. In fact, I'd like you to stop reading and walk to the nearest mirror. Look into it and say to that beautiful face that's reflected there, "God chose me, and He loves me. He will never give up on me."

Are you in the middle of an imprisonment right now? Maybe you found it impossible to let go of your false gods last week. Maybe you couldn't because of a relationship or emotional ties.

If this is you, take heart. Satan often interferes the most when he sees you actively moving in the right direction. So as difficult as it is to make the change, as many obstacles as darkness threw into your path, count it all for joy, just like Paul. Know that you tried, and you will keep trying. Just as God didn't give up on you, you'll never give up on Him.

My friend Melanie had to leave her husband of eight years, a hard-core alcoholic, in order to regain her faith and restore her relationship with God. I was with her through most of the ordeal. "It took everything in me just to leave," she said. "It's like there is nothing left."

She carried around the awfulness, the betrayal, and the lies in her head for a long time. She looked and acted completely empty. Drained. She moved in the wrong direction for a couple of years—*years!*—before she was finally able to put some of her imprisonment behind her and live in the present.

Please write about last week's experience of giving up a functional god/idol, and what it felt like to you. You can do it here or in a journal.

_____

_____

_____

_____

_____

_____

_____

_____

Remembering that imprisonment can be emotional, relational, or many other things besides physically sitting in a jail cell, answer thee questions:

Are you now or have you ever been imprisoned? _____

Do you feel that Jesus loves you now? _____

Did you feel His love during your imprisonment? _____

_____

Day 2: Divine or De-vine?

ODAY WE'RE GOING TO TALK about pruning. If you have ever had to prune a vine or bush to make it grow better, you will know exactly what Jesus is referring to in the book of John. I used to hate it when my dad and my great-aunt told me to prune or pinch back my plants. Sometimes I didn't do it. I hated to "waste" any part of their beautiful, green foliage and flowers. I felt as if I was hurting the plants.

Eventually, however, I learned that pruning leads to more growth and also to thicker, bushier plants. It makes them grow the way we want them to. Now I have a bed full of roses, and I regularly trim them back. They thrive so much that lots of passersby stop to ask how I do it. Well, I should tell them I read John, chapter 15. I finally learned that pruning is necessary if you want something to grow right. In a sense, you're training it to go the way you want it to. That's how we are pruned by God. He shows us how to grow in the right direction, and sometimes it's a little painful.

I found out recently that if grapevines are left to grow on their own, they'll have lots of beautiful green foliage but no fruit. They require a professional, a master vinedresser, to clip them just right so they produce the best kind of grapes. He prunes off all those little bits that grew up through their own strength, leaving only the parts that are important. That is *exactly* what Jesus does—if we let Him.

Please open your Bible to John, chapter 15, and read verses 1–8.

We see that there are two kinds of branches. The first kind is not bearing fruit. Those branches are cut off. Verse 6 says those branches are "picked up, thrown into the fire and burned."

The other kind of branch is carefully lifted up from the mud by the vinedresser (God) who realizes that there is no sunlight down there in the mud. These branches are carefully cleaned and pruned. Perhaps they are tied to others so they remain upright where they can receive more sunlight. The fruit they bear are the good spiritual fruits that flow from Jesus—the vine and the divine—through the branches, His people. Us!

List some truths about yourself (the branch) that you find in these verses:

_____

_____

_____

_____

The Greek word for *prune* is also used for *clean*. Does it make a difference to you that Jesus might be "cleaning" you rather than pruning you?

_____

Remember, what is important is not what the pruning means to you. It's what it means to God—the One who loves you. Yet these times of pruning are when we hear people say, "See? God doesn't care about us. He allows all this hurt."

Jesus speaks with understanding about the pain we will suffer as we are pruned. Suffering is part of every believer's life. But the suffering is not some careless hacking with a set of pruning shears. Rather it is carefully, thoughtfully done, one tiny branchlet at a time, by a master vinedresser.

My roses suffered a setback this spring. Just when the buds were all there, and tons of them were just waiting to burst into bloom (and I'm pretty sure they yell "spring!" as they do it), we had a semifrost. Not bad enough to cover them up, though we did that one night too. We left them to the elements on this particular night, and all those hopeful little buds turned black and flopped over. That meant that until I, the gardener, got out there and did some gentle pruning, nothing was going to happen. Had I taken the shears out and angrily cut the branches to the ground, we'd have had no flowers all season. God doesn't whack us to the ground, nor does He leave us with our heads bowed down. Like those roses, He sees that we're trying to grow. His pruning still hurts, but it's the gentle kind. Frankly I removed some of my rosebuds carefully with my fingertips. Do you ever feel the fingertips of God brushing your face?

Sometimes you have to do your own kind of pruning too. Have you ever met someone who seemed bent on finding the negative in every situation? Some people seem determined to be like Eeyore, the donkey who was friends with Winnie the Pooh. Do you remember him? He was so dreary that even his house was called "Eeyore's Gloomy Place: Rather Boggy and Sad," Poor fellow!

The Eeyores of this world haven't learned yet to "count it all joy." If you find they pull you downward, it may be best to limit your time with them, to prune them away, at least for a while during this study. That way you can root out your annoying little gods without the bogginess or the sadness taking over.

Please finish today by reading John 15:9–17. Write comments here:

Day 3: Our Source of Security

PLEASE START TODAY BY READING 1 Kings 3:1–15 in your favorite version of the Bible or online.

King Solomon had a chance to ask for whatever he wanted. He could have had fame, fortune, many wives—anything at all. But part of Solomon's job was to make life-altering decisions when the people came to him for advice. So Solomon asked God for discernment (v. 9). God was so pleased! In fact, God gave Solomon the wealth he *didn't* ask for because he was so happy that Solomon had chosen wisdom and discernment as his gift.

I like to think that Solomon chose wisdom because he had his eye on the things of God. Perhaps Solomon recognized what we generally don't realize today, that God is all around us. Maybe he just didn't own an iPad. He was able to focus on the good, the eternal.

We, on the other hand, are so overcome with our gadgets, devices, distractions, etc. that we are not as able to focus on the things of God. Perhaps we've forgotten about the Garden of Eden, where God Himself walked around with Adam and Eve. Perhaps we're simply unable to grasp the greatness of a Lord who is all around us. *Perhaps our idol is security.*

Where do we find security? We have a great tendency to trust in the rules of religion rather than have faith in a person and our relationship with Him. We'd rather follow those rules—and judge people who don't—than nurture the communication we have with Jesus. It's much easier to agree not to steal (something that didn't hold a whole lot of appeal anyway) than to agree to meet Him quietly every morning. It is easier to go through the motions than to open our hearts. After all, who knows what God might do if we actually let Him all the way in? Send us to Africa? *I don't have a passport.* Make us sell all our worldly possessions? *I really, really love my collection of high heels.* Tell me to go serve in the soup kitchen downtown? *I'd rather just sit silently in church on Sunday morning, thank you.*

My security was in the Baptist church, so when God called me to serve in the United Methodist church for a time, I said, "No, thank you." He clearly and immediately said, "Go!" So, head hanging, I went. I still don't know why He sent me there, but I was obedient. For once. I found many new loving friends, learned a lot about leadership, and the first devotional I ever had published was in the United Methodist publication *The Upper Room.* Not bad for simply saying yes to God.

Success is one thing that can give us a false sense of security. I call it false because by becoming successful, we start to think we can operate under our own power. Success for you might mean a great job, a huge rambling house, a big family, or lots of money. It could mean working hard to build up your retirement fund. Remember, *if you've begun to obsess over it*, it's a functional god. A little-g god. The real God usually fades into the background in a life like this.

The book of Amos shows how harshly God judges His people when they place their confidence in idols instead of God. Israel was not following God's law (dare I say, *again*). The year was about 750 BC. Amos, a simple farmer, was a prophet who foretold what would happen to Israel for their disobedience. He condemned the Israelites in a fiery speech about their moral collapse, religious apostasy, and political corruption. Still, the people were secure in their wealth, power, and position. They "knew" that God would not destroy them—after all, their kingdom housed the temple. Could we apply any of this erroneous, false confidence to today's world?

May I suggest that perhaps the people also looked down their noses at Amos? He, a mere farmer, was telling them, the powerful ones, to watch their backs. Imagine the gossip!

One of the most important teachings from Amos is that God is the one who provides. God wanted to give them everything. Sadly the people were confident enough in themselves that they refused to budge. Within another generation, the Assyrians had overtaken them.

Are there things in your life that God might want to give you, but you have stubbornly kept Him out of some part of your life? What part are you keeping to yourself for your own false sense of security?

_____

_____

Would you describe yourself as having more security in following the rules, or in practicing grace? Why?

_____

_____

What parts of your life give you security? (These don't have to be things. They can be anything you see, hear, touch, or feel.)

_____

_____

Day 4: Press On

REMEMBER AT THE BEGINNING OF this week when we discussed Paul sitting in prison—and feeling overjoyed about it? Paul was secure in Jesus Christ. That's what made him able to feel so happy. He gladly became a servant of Christ in order to have true security.

Now, lest you think that Paul had been down on his luck or was a frequent prison visitor, let's remember. In the beginning his name was Saul. He was a Roman citizen, a second-generation Pharisee. As Saul, he had money, power, status, a sense of belonging, and a zeal for persecuting the saints. In today's language, we'd call him successful. After his conversion, he gladly gave up everything he was and everything he knew in order to become one of those very ones he'd persecuted. He went to prison . . . and sang hymns to God while he was there.

I read an interesting study about success. It said if people believe they achieve success by winning, then they tend to envy those people they perceive as having more. But people who think success is earned will work a lot harder to get it. And might I add, you will be prouder of your own success if you feel you've earned it.

However, success, especially in today's shaky economy, can be instantly taken away. People have lost jobs, homes, and in some cases everything they own. We've had tornadoes and devastating hurricanes wipe out possessions. If success is measured by "things," many Americans are hurting. If you have ever used the phrase "self-made man" to describe you or your loved ones, you could be shaken to the core in a heartbeat.

Fortunately, it's not really that way at all. We aren't "self-made." We don't design who we are.

Please read Ephesians 2:8–10.

We are saved by _____ .

We were created by God as His _____ .

Such wonderful and familiar verses. But sometimes when a verse is familiar, we don't dig deep into ourselves and really pay attention. So I'd like to ask you to read it again in another version:

> It's God's gift from start to finish! We don't play the major role. If we did, we'd probably go around bragging that we'd done the whole thing! No, we neither make nor save ourselves. God does both the making and saving. He creates each of us by Christ Jesus to join him in the work he does, the good work he has gotten ready for us to do, work we had better be doing. (Ephesians 2:8–10 MSG)

Who are you in Christ? _____

What special gifts has he given you to use for the good of his kingdom?

_____

Name other gifts God has given you lately, whether answered prayers, epiphanies, moments, etc.: _____

_____

Consider memorizing this verse:

> Not that I have already obtained this or am already perfect, but I press on to make it my own, because Christ Jesus has made me his own. (Philippians 3:12 ESV)

Day 5: Down in the Valley

EVERYONE GOES THROUGH WHAT I call "valley experiences" in their lives. A difficult time. You know, "Yea, though I walk through the valley . . ." We understand that suffering is a part of life, yet when things get difficult, we wonder why God is allowing us to suffer. Sometimes we wonder if God has abandoned us.

God's Word reminds us that He is always there to love and guide us. He protects us. Every bad experience He allows is part of His greater plan for us. In fact, we learn much more in the valley than we do on the mountaintop. Maybe that's the whole point.

When you feel like you're in the bottom of the valley, it is important to remember that it's *only a passageway*, not a destination. You aren't going to stay there forever unless it's by your own choice. Psalm 23:4 says, "I walk through the darkest valley." It doesn't say "I sit in the valley for months a time . . . holding pity parties . . . woe is me!"

How do we end up in the valley? Well, there are many reasons. We may have lost our position, our dream, or a person. We may be experiencing spiritual warfare. It might be an action by God or by other people's behavior or even a result of our own misbehavior. Regardless, we can feel terrible pain—pain that shatters.

Many times we respond to the valley in negative ways. We think our valley is a tunnel that doesn't end and has no light. We lose hope, perhaps even considering suicide. I know I promised that this week we would stay in the loving arms of Jesus. The reason I'm bringing up the valley is because we don't always handle it in the best way. Jesus is still holding us in His loving arms when we're in the midst of a trial, but sometimes we forget. There are also bound to be some of us participating in this study who are going through the valley right now.

Here are a few reasons we might not handle the valley experience very well:

» We don't know God's Word. Only through Scripture can we find the reassurance we need to move through this sort of trial.

» Our belief system is not solid yet.

» We don't understand God's ways. This goes back to number 1, knowing His Word. In the Bible we find many examples of saints who suffered, even though they may have been completely faithful to God.

» Our faith is shallow.

» We haven't moved our idol yet.

Do any of these ring true for you? _____

If so, jot down a few things you can do to make a change—hopefully before your next valley experience! We won't be sharing this in class, so write from the heart.

_____

_____

My personal problem with the valley is my impatience. I want it over with *now*! But God is always more interested in our character than our comfort. He wants us to surrender to Him. So resisting His work may lengthen the time we're in the valley. We want out—in fact, we want to run through as fast as we can go. But God is content to leave us there for our own good, like leaving a child in time-out. He wants to change our thinking over to His perspective. So if you're in a really deep valley, you know that God can do some equally deep work, if you will let Him.

It is also possible to become stuck in the valley. God's truth is available to protect us and comfort us, but that doesn't mean we will use it. We can be like the sheep that strays in spite of the shepherd's best efforts. We can be stubborn and resistant to forward motion.

During these hard times we can figure out how to rely on God instead of our stuff, our idol. That's what this study is all about. In the valley we come face-to-face with the nature of God. As we feel our pain, we feel His presence. As we feel our loss, we feel His love.

The last time you were in a valley, did you feel God's presence? How?

_____

Next time you're in the valley, try to look at it in a new light. It means God's up to something in your life, and that's exciting! Seek Him out and simply ask Him what is important. Thank Him for bringing you through the valley, even before He does, and acknowledge that He always has a purpose.

Romans 8:28 says, "And we know that in all things God works for the good of those who love him, who have been called according to his purpose." [Yes, even the valleys!]

Please take some time to look up the following verses. You may have a few favorites of your own to add. Circle the one that makes you feel most loved.

John 3:16–17   **1 Peter 5:7**

John 13:6, 7   **Galatians 5:22-24**

John 15:13   **1 Corinthians 13**

Responsibilities of Salvation
(How to Remain Pruned)

Blessed is the one who perseveres under trial because, having stood the test, that person
will receive the crown of life that the Lord has promised to those who love him.
—James 1:12

W E'RE GOING TO DO A lot of Bible reading this week. Along with the beauty
and hope of salvation comes a lot of responsibility. We need to explore those
responsibilities. Remember though, His yoke is easy and His burden is light.

I hope that as you have begun to clear out the false gods, you're feeling more peaceful
and loved. Remember that you may experience spiritual warfare (Satan loves to kick us back
down if we're on the way up). Pray that you will see it for what it is, and take heart in spite
of the difficulties.

One problem that often occurs when you've cleared out a false god is you realize there
are two or three more. That's okay—they are usually cousins (you stopped admiring your
own car and house, and now you realize you have just as much love for your clothing; or you
stopped gaming so much, and discovered now you're on Facebook two or three hours a day).
Just back up and deal with the next one. And remember, it only becomes a god if it gets in

the way of your worship of the Lord. It's a misshapen desire, a like gone wrong. But you are in control, not the "thing" that is driving you. Push it back to its rightful place.

I have a 125-gallon fish tank (it's six feet long, just to give you an idea of the size). It's full of plants, like an underwater garden. Because I constantly fertilize and inject CO_2 to help it grow, it constantly needs pruning. Sometimes I just trim back some tiny bits; other times I have to chop a plant way back to reshape it or to improve its growth habit. Sometimes I have to cut off all the roots and let it create new ones. Like plants, we began allowing ourselves to be pruned in week 4. This week helps us stay that way.

Day 1: Rejoice in Who You Are

PROBLEMS, PAIN, AND PERSECUTION CAN steal our peace and shred apart our faith. Christians were not popular in the Roman Empire during the AD 60s—even less popular than we are now. They were slandered, robbed, and threatened. They faced discrimination of every kind. They were afraid and suffering.

Peter's first letter reminded them, as it does us, of their identity—we are royalty! Peter says that believers can trust and rejoice even when we have pain, because we are never without hope. Our society may be questioning who we are as believers, as Christians, but you already know who you are—His chosen one, His beloved, a priest, and part of His holy nation.

Please read 1 Peter 1:3–12.

Verse 5 says we are shielded by God's power through our _____ .

Your genuine faith will result in: _____

_____

_____(v. 7).

Write the last sentence of verse 12 here:

_____

What do you think it means?

_____

This letter from Peter emphasizes the anticipation that belongs only to those who have made a choice of salvation. We are not promised an easy life, but rather a living hope. In between becoming a believer and receiving our final reward, we experience many trials. But many of us get in a habit of turning our attention to the bad things that have happened in our lives instead of lifting our face to that sure promise.

How much of your Christian life have you spent focused on the bad—rebellion, jealousy, materialism—your time-stealers, obsessions, or idols? Do you waste time looking back and dwelling on past failures or disappointments? How much time did that leave for Christ?

God is not Santa, the fulfiller of the wish list, but He is the Lord of hope. Hope in Christ is your anchor (see Hebrews 6:19–20). If your anchor isn't in Him, you will flounder around, going through life like a boat with no rudder. Allow the Holy Spirit to fill you with this living hope. Let yourself be guided into God's arms.

Please read Lamentations 3:22–24.

Because of his love, we will not be _____ .

As Christians, we are self-confident because of who we are in Christ. God lives in us, giving us a special power to use only for good that comes from Him. That means we can have discernment, wisdom, love, joy, and peace—and more—all because of Him.

If you have not felt self-confident, or haven't been happy with who you are up until now, realize that none of us are perfect. The grass is truly not greener on the other side. As Paul told us in Philippians 4:11, "I am not saying this because I am in need, *for I have learned to be content whatever the circumstances*" (emphasis added).

Please read the following verses:

> It's in Christ that we find out who we are and what we are living for. Long before we first heard of Christ and got our hopes up, he had his eye on us, had designs on us for glorious living, part of the overall purpose he is working out in everything and everyone. (Ephesians 1:11–12 MSG)

When does it say Christ had His eye on us? _____

Compare the above to John 15:16 in whichever translation you prefer.

_____

Do these verses help you remember that God chose you "before"? *Before* you got into that relationship . . . *before* you developed that bad habit . . . *before* you made a promise you didn't keep. He knew what was going to happen and He *chose us anyway*. He's a merciful king. He is solidly yours. He wants to delight in us, and us in Him.

If God rejoices in who you are, how much more you can rejoice. He isn't waiting for the cleaned-up, slicked-up, date-night version of you. He's just waiting for the real you!

Day 2: Walk in Holiness

D o YOU FEEL THAT YOU could never be truly holy because of things you've done or where your false gods have led you? If so—good! Because today I'm going to shatter those false notions.

Please read Psalm 33:20–22.

> The Lord wants us to focus on Him, and if we do, the negatives fall away. By handing over all your worries and difficulties—imagine yourself giving Him all of them—you can truly look into His face and "turn your eyes upon Jesus," as the song says.
>
> We wouldn't chase rainbows—false gods—if we didn't think they would give us something. Unfortunately they don't give us anything other than false hope. The Holy Spirit fills us with a living hope.

What does your false god give to you? _____

How could you receive the same thing, be fulfilled the same way, without your false god? By turning to God instead?

_____

Have you ever done something totally off the wall because somebody threatened your false god/idol? _____

What was it? _____

One man tells the story of being robbed. He arrived home at his tiny trailer to find it had been broken into—his television, stereo, and shotgun were missing, his most valuable possessions. His body surged with anger as he thought about getting revenge on the thieves, hurting or even killing them if he could find them. Luckily he never did. Later in life, he became filled with remorse as he realized he had let "things" become the center of his life.

Some people feel that their salvation can be questioned because of wickedness by their parent or another relative. They believe they will never truly accomplish holiness. Or the opposite—they believe they already have the Holy Spirit because their parents do, so they've somehow inherited it. Or because they have always been in church. This is completely wrong thinking. The Bible has many passages about our *individual* responsibility to be holy. For example:

> Anyone who listens to the word but does not do what it says is like someone who looks at his face in a mirror and, after looking at himself, goes away and immediately forgets what he looks like. But whoever looks intently into the perfect law that gives freedom, and continues in it—not forgetting what they have heard, but doing it—they will be blessed in what they do. (James 1:23–25 MSG)

Please read 1 Peter 1:13–2:3 (NASB).

Prepare your minds for _____ . What sort of action is Peter referring to?

_____

This is the first of four instructions Peter gives us for walking in holiness. True holiness is both internal and external. There is always a need for balance in life, and part of that balance is between who we say we are and what we do. Just as Jesus is chosen, we are chosen. Because of our part of the royal priesthood, we must take the call to walk in holiness as our highest and best calling.

Holiness requires that we take our eyes off our surroundings, problems, worries, and relationships. It requires that we look only into Jesus' beautiful face. This is how we bring honor to Him.

By the grace of God, holy living is possible. He has given us the blood of Christ in order to forgive our sin. He has given us the Holy Spirit to free us from sin. He has also given us instructions as to how to live in a way that pleases Him. So we have to do our part.

One aspect of God's forgiveness means *no guilt*. I say this especially to mothers. We moms have a particular talent for feeling guilty long after we have been forgiven. Don't go there. Guilt pulls little bits of your holy self away every time you give in to it.

Peter's second instruction is to be self-controlled. This means to keep our spiritual life in check by rejecting the world's sinful system. Believers' goals should be in line with God's goals—winning others to Christ so they too can have the living hope, and so that we all can praise and glorify God together.

Next, Peter tells us to fix our hope on God's _____ .

He is commanding us to hope. In the thesaurus, synonyms for *hope* are words like *desire*, *expectation*, and *belief*.[8] God is not delighted when we perform for Him like actors or acrobats; rather, He is delighted when we have faith that is based on Him, what He can do for us in His strength. He wants us to hope fully for that. Not "hope mostly, and doubt a little," but hope with our entire soul. Wait with expectation that lives fully in His grace. This way, grace gets all the glory!

Please read Psalm 147:10–11.

Based on verse 11, do you believe the Lord delights in you?

_____

Read 1 Peter 1:14, then Romans 12:2. Both Peter and Paul encourage us to be different from the world. Not only our actions but also our attitudes. We live by different rules because we are under the will of God.

Can you list a few ways you are different from the world around you?

_____

_____

_____

Finally, we must be holy. The Holy Spirit lives in us, and so we are called to love and serve God. In everything we do, we need to glorify Him. Every action that you do can be done to the glory of God.

Years ago, I played in orchestra concerts all the time. At each concert before the first downbeat I would lower my head and pray that somehow God would use that music for His glory. One night in a great moment of doubt, I looked up at the thousands of people in the audience and wondered how on earth could they be blessed through this concert, through only one player's prayer?

But it wasn't up to me to choose how they could receive the blessing. My only responsibility was to do everything—even playing my viola—to the glory of God. First Corinthians 10:31 says that even eating and drinking can be done to the glory of God. If that is true, surely so can music.

What are some things you can start doing to the glory of God this week?

1. _____

2. _____

3. _____

Please read 1 Thessalonians 4:1–12.

List a few of the instructions given in this verse.

_____

_____

_____

_____

How can you incorporate those in your life this week?

_____

_____

_____

One of the first things I realized when I read 1 Thessalonians is that God never mentions ignorance as an excuse for not doing the things He wants us to do. We don't have to call on ignorance; we can call on the Holy Spirit.

As believers, walking in holiness includes loving one another, but at the same time minding our own business. Look again at 1 Thessalonians 4:9–12. Don't you just love the way God knows us so well that He can guess what we might do? We've discussed before being busybodies in the name of Christianity. These verses remind us that just won't do.

Day 3: Watch for Drift

PART OF OUR RESPONSIBILITY IS to keep an eye out for signs of drifting, both in ourselves and in those around us. We went over this in detail in week 2, but now that we are actively removing false gods, it's important enough to mention again. People who remove their idol can easily start to drift.

Remember that you have never done anything so bad that you cannot return to the arms of Jesus. Sin is merely turning your back on God for a while; all you have to do is turn back around. Yes, we all figured out that we had a functional god. Or three. So what? At least we found it out while we were still on this earth—in time to push it away, in time to ask for forgiveness and get back on track.

I find that people who are hurting badly carry guilt, whether warranted or not, and feel they cannot return to God. I think that is because there is true guilt—the godly kind, conviction—and false guilt. True guilt is a warning sign that we are in sin and need to repent. But after the cleansing, you can rest assured that Christ's open arms are waiting for you. He wants nothing more than your presence. If you still are covered with guilt, it's now a false guilt. He absolutely does not want you to hang back there in the false guilt, barely able to function. Clear out the guilt and make room for the renewing love of God!

I just finished visiting with a friend from way back in the past. We have literally known each other all our lives. We were both raised in church, though different churches in a small town. Her parents were strict—you could say they lived the Old Testament way, believing Christianity was something you were supposed to do and act, and you had to dress the part. Somewhere along the way, perhaps due to this strictness, she began to drift. And when she drifted, she went a really long way. It took many years for me to realize how far. Then it took a few more to have the opportunity to address it with her.

Today I met with her to try to pull her back. I talked with friends about this meeting ahead of time and planned what to say. I carried along a Bible verse on a little note card, which she did accept. We talked candidly about her life.

"I know what I did was wrong," she remarked.

Right after she said it, I could see the wall go up over her eyes. To me, people are either open to the gospel or closed. She had shut down her heart.

"But it doesn't matter! Jesus is about love and grace—and mercy. You can change *now*," I insisted.

By the end of our two-hour conversation, her position had not changed. She understands that I love her, but she is closed to the idea of letting the Lord help her change her life. She won't go to counseling or to a wonderful group I know of called Celebrate Recovery. She didn't want the Bible I offered her. She "knows she can change herself." I know that means change isn't going to take place. I came home feeling drained and sad.

Sometimes God allows us to fail, and always He allows us free will. He let my friend choose—and she did not choose Him.

Please read Jeremiah 29:13.

Has there been a time in your life when you had to seek Him with all your heart? Describe that time and how it felt to seek God.

_____

_____

Now turn to Jeremiah 17:10. The Lord will search the _____ and test the

_____ .

Please read Zechariah 13:9.

Please write the next-to-last line here: "I will say, '_____ .'"

A long time ago there was a wonderful book about Jesus waiting for you in your home. It described each room of the house in great detail, and how Jesus sat in a chair day after day, waiting for you to show up, whether you did or not. Well, He's still there! So as you watch out for signs of drift, keep in mind that He is always there, no matter what you've done. He already knows we're going to sin. It's the step we take next that matters.

Day 4: Trust in Right Things

WHERE DO YOU PUT YOUR trust? Do you trust your husband? Your pastor? Your best friend? Do you trust God with all your heart?

It is easy to say and even believe that we trust God entirely. But too many of us don't trust Him enough to give Him access to our entire selves. It's interesting that we can be betrayed by friends, husbands, and even pastors, but we will never be betrayed by the Lord of the universe. Yet that is who we hold back from.

Please read Proverbs 3:5–6.

He will make our paths_____.

List some positive experiences you have had that let you know you can trust God with all your heart.

_____

_____

_____

Trust in God means letting Him into all our deepest, darkest places. Holding back often means there's still a functional god roaming around. Trust means that when we ask, "Why me?" we can answer the question biblically.

Please read 1 Corinthians 10:13. To me, this verse says that God is in control, and that God will not let Satan press me further than I can bear.

What does it say to you? _____

_____

When you become doubtful about fully trusting God to provide your needs, make a mindful choice to reject discouraging words. Opposition and discouragement often come from the people who matter most to us: friends and family. Since we believe them to be on our side, we are hesitant to reject what they say.

But when you are sure that your walk is godly, you can be just as sure that Satan is simply using that person as a tool to get what he wants. Behind every challenge is a spiritual battle. You must choose whether to allow yourself to be discouraged or walk in victory with God. You will come out the winner if your trust is in the right place.

Please read Psalm 37:5–6 and Proverbs 3:5.

Comment: _____

A lot of people spend their whole lives unable to fully trust in God, unable to hand over every fiber of their being to His care. I believe this is because trust is a verb. It's something you have to do actively. But many of us treat trust passively. We give it lip service and not much else.

When you choose to trust God, you choose that *every* event, *every* moment, *every* encounter is a part of His divine plan. By choosing to trust, you are continually renewing your belief that God is unshakably trustworthy.

Do you wholly trust God? If not, the Holy Spirit knows us better than we know ourselves, so He will give us exactly what we need to make this change. He will help you to create this trust—to change it into a powerful verb that in turn changes your life. He will let you do this in tiny steps if you need to. He'll catch you when you fall and rejoice with you when you succeed.

It is true that trusting God will not always bring you blatant, immediate victory. Sometimes you will have failures and disappointments. Sometimes you will lose. All of the time, we don't know what tomorrow will bring. But a life lived in total trust gives glory to God and blesses that life beyond measure. And a life filled with God is one great big adventure!

Day 5: Pruning for Humility

PLEASE READ PHILIPPIANS 2:3–8. THESE verses say that Christ took on some characteristics. List them here.

_____

_____

_____

_____

I hope that one of the things you listed was obedience. Do we have the wherewithal to be obedient to the point of death? Some of us do. I remember during the Columbine shootings, one of the attackers asked if anyone was a Christian. A young girl said, "I am."

He promptly killed her.

I've wondered ever since, if I were in her situation, would I raise my hand and identify myself as a Christian?

Besides imitating Christ's obedience, Philippians tells us we are also to have His humility. Other words for humility might be *modesty*, *meekness*, *humbleness*, and *submission*.

When Christ knew that He had to be obedient to death on the cross, Peter immediately argued with Him.

Please turn to Matthew 16:23.

What did Jesus say to Peter? _____

_____

Peter had to give up his own desires. Jesus was telling him not to be selfish. Peter wanted Jesus to remain as a king on earth, but it couldn't happen. Peter attained greatness because he humbled himself and submitted to God's will.

Any time we submit to God's will, we allow His light to shine through us. We may not understand why we must let go of our obsession, or why we are entering a certain season or difficulty, but what we can do is allow the situation to make us humble. That is what Peter did. In 1 Peter 5, we see that he had learned his lesson well, and went on to teach it to others around him.

To put our joy in our own strength, wisdom, pleasures, or comforts is to idolize these things instead of God. To delight in the Lord as He delights in us is an act of worship. First Corinthians 1:31 says, "Therefore, as it is written: 'Let the one who boasts boast in the Lord.'"

Sometimes our boasting is not in the Lord, because we relish our belongings. Whether we speak of it or not, we may hold on to a person, place, or thing that we truly love. This prevents us from humbleness.

But holding on to things can really keep us from being a branch of the vine, Jesus (see John 15). Sometimes it can be downright dangerous. I heard a story once about some monkeys out in the jungle. Some scientists were trying to catch the monkeys in order to study them, but the creatures were difficult to trap. After trying several different methods, the scientists set out some big wooden boxes containing nuts (monkeys apparently love to eat nuts). Each box had a small hole cut in the side, just large enough for the monkey to reach into. When the monkey stuck his hand in and closed it around a nut, his fist was too big to pull back out through the hole. So he sat still, and allowed himself to be caught rather than let go of the prize—the nut.

What kind of nut might you be holding on to? Is it fair to say that we trade our freedom for the prizes we want to hold on to? Perhaps we are comfortable with our old self, old way of doing things, habits, belongings, a bad relationship, or a less-than-satisfying job.

This monkey story really resonated with me. As I'm writing this, we're cleaning out our house. You can bet I have a lot to let go of—years of kids' artwork and stories, three closets of clothing. I'm also the sort of person who likes to get into a habit or routine and stay there, perhaps even when it isn't working so well. I hang on to the nut long after it's decayed and rotted and of no use whatsoever. This could come from sheer stubbornness or from a belief that letting go will not allow my circumstances to change.

If we do let go, we have freedom. But then we have to make a behavioral change. With freedom always comes responsibility. Which do you choose: freedom with some healthy responsibility? Or a life of misery, enslavement, and imprisonment?

What do you hold on to today, finding it difficult to let go? _____

_____

To what and to whom are you bound? _____

_____

Are you willing to give it up? Let it go? Throw it down? _____

How can you begin to let go?

_____

_____

_____

Father, I pray that each and every one of us has the insight, courage, and strength to make the changes we need in order to be in your will. Amen.

Staying Idol Free in an Idolatrous World

*And the peace of God, which transcends all understanding, will
guard your hearts and your minds in Christ Jesus.*
—Philippians 4:7

KEEPING IDOLS, FALSE GODS, AND functional gods out of our lives will be easier going forward, because now we know what to look for. During the original focus group for this study, we had people make all sorts of changes, decisions, and adjustments to help their spiritual lives become the main thing.

Those false gods will continue to try to move in though, so we must be on our guard at all times. Not in a fear-based way. I'm not saying everyone should cringe and tremble inside their homes for fear of what lurks outside the door. Rather we must be cheerfully alert and aware of what's going on. Life is about balance, and it is up to us to keep our own scale evenly weighted.

Day 1: Be the Real Deal

AVE YOU BEEN A HYPOCRITE at times? If we are honest, we'd all admit we have been. Yet walking with Christ means living the same inside as outside, and vice versa. If something is wrong according to God's Word, it's wrong—period. Don't play around with it. Don't invite Satan to lunch by messing with things that, if you took an honest inventory, you know are wrong.

Keeping a holy frame of mind and a pure heart means you've got to have confidence, a belief in yourself in how the Holy Spirit can work through you. Recognize negative feelings, if you have them, and remember Philippians 4:13: "I can do all this through him who gives me strength."

Part of that confidence is more than just avoiding the negatives, it is also embracing the positive. When I was a young Christian, I would talk about Jesus or Christianity, but only if the other person started the conversation. When I realized that it is our job to help save the lost, and what a serious assignment that is, I began to pray for the strength to be the one to start the conversations. As an introvert, starting any sort of conversation was hard for me—especially that one! But it got easier.

Years later, when my husband and I owned our joint music store (me) and antiques business (him), I had become a lot more comfortable in my skin—my Christian skin, that is. It seemed God sent people into our store on purpose with whom we could talk about Jesus. Sometimes it was because they needed to talk about a problem. Sometimes we'd just share the joy of the Lord. Occasionally I could tell that we were witnessing to someone who needed to hear it. You never know what seed you might have planted, but you'll never be wrong by talking about Christ.

Please read John 14:27.

A real Christian experiences _____ .

How much of the time do you feel peaceful? In today's busy society, it is easy to feel overwhelmed and anything but peaceful. Yet the peace of God, once you finally achieve it, truly is a peace that "surpasses all understanding" (Philippians 4:7 ESV).

Those who walk the walk do not play around with immorality, lying, dishonesty, or other sins. In fact, they're on guard at all times to avoid those sins. When you came to Christ, He forgave your sins and purified your heart. That didn't mean you became holier than everyone around you, but rather it made you more aware of how far we all really are from the holiness of Jesus.

In spite of this, we still are able to lead a peaceful and righteous life. We can avoid the sins mentioned above and attempt to have a life that is pure. If we have integrity, it will be validated by what we say and what we do. Pure in heart means we can also be pure in action. People with integrity act in ways that clearly line up with their heart values.

Mark Twain said, "If you tell the truth you don't have to remember anything."[9]

Please read Matthew 5:8.

A real Christian strives for _____ .

A soldier following the leadership of a great commander willingly obeys every order. Remember the story in Matthew of the centurion who asked Jesus to heal his servant? He told Jesus that it wasn't necessary to actually come to his home. This man knew that only a word from Jesus would get the results he desired. He knew this because of his job as a soldier. Soldiers do exactly what they are told.

In the same way, a real Christian gives over all control to the Lord. We agree to do what He wants us to do and go where He wants us to go. We don't care what the cost is. We don't give him 90 percent, thinking to hold on to 10 percent for ourselves. We are blessed when we give 100 percent.

Please read Proverbs 3:5–6.

The real Christian obeys, because he has _____ in God.

Most of all, if we're the real deal, we practice love. Not the somewhat exploited meaning that is often given to love, which describes using someone for our own selfish purposes or satisfaction. True love wants only the best for the other person, and puts his or her needs above our own.

Some months before I began working on this book, the Lord told me I needed to learn how to love people better. It has been an interesting journey, and one I'm still working on. I look at people and think *He loves them, so I should too.* I try to find people to pray for who aren't my usual suspects—people outside the circle of family, friends who are going through difficulty, etc. I look at people and wonder how to love them more. Those around me probably wonder why I study them so intently.

I'll share with you just one of the big changes I've made. Through my lifetime, I have never attended funerals. There are several reasons; the biggest one is that I pick up the emotions of everyone around me, so in such a sad situation I can hardly bear it. I literally choke up from the moment I enter the room, and it kicks my fibromyalgia into high gear. Then I'm exhausted the rest of the day from carrying around all those extra feelings. But funerals are for the living loved ones left behind, not for the person who died. So one way I can love people is by showing up.

Just yesterday we attended visitation for a family who lost their twenty-one-year-old daughter. They are a loving, Christian family, people you're just happy to be around. We stood in line to speak to them so long it was time for the funeral to begin, so they were sent out to the parlor. We were still at the far back of the church, about hundredth in line.

Normally . . . well, normally I wouldn't have even been there. But I really felt I was there for the other daughter, the one who had lost her only sibling. She was my violin student when she was in high school, and a good one. We'd even performed some together. I always love and pray for my students. I know what boys they like and what their math grades are. And in the strange twist that has accompanied us ever since we met nearly five years ago, my husband, Mickey, knew this family too. So when we realized we weren't going to get a chance to speak to them, Mickey and I snuck around and went into the parlor. The funeral director normally won't let people in like that—he guards the door with passion—but somehow his back was turned and we got right by him. See how good God is? We were able to speak with the father, and I was able to hold on to that girl, stroke her hair, look into her eyes, and tell her I love her.

This all reminded me that the way of Jesus Christ is the way of pure love, and that's what we are supposed to emulate. Even when faced with difficulty, we have to find a way to love the people around us. Even when it makes us uncomfortable or exhausted. Even when they are acting stupid. Even when they don't love us back. Because we don't love in order to get something; we love to share love.

Please read the following three verses:

John 13:35
Romans 8:39
1 John 4:7–11

The real Christian has ＿＿＿＿＿＿＿＿＿＿＿＿＿＿＿＿＿ .

Please read the following verses:

John 15:13
Proverbs 17:17
Proverbs 18:24

Do you have friends like those described in these verses? _____

Are you the friend described in the verses? _____

A discussion of love is incomplete if we do not mention the love chapter, 1 Corinthians 13. If you have time, read it through three times this week.

Day 2: Act Like God Is Watching

THERE'S A BEAUTIFUL LAKE IN Canada called Lake Louise. Surrounded by mountains and glaciers, both of which contribute to its beauty, the lake is famous mainly for its unusual turquoise-colored waters. What many don't realize is that the color is created by the movement of the glaciers, which grind the limestone rocks underneath into a fine powder. The limestone is then carried into the lake by the water, turning it blue. The seemingly insignificant movement from the glaciers is responsible for the incredible beauty. Without the movement, this lake that so many visitors come to see would be just another oversized pond in the mountains.

Likewise the seemingly unimportant actions we take can reap wonderful rewards later. I had a rose garden in front of my previous home, where there was a great deal of motor vehicle traffic. An anonymous letter came in January one year telling me how much I "contributed to the beauty of this earth with my little patch of flowers." It probably didn't mean a whole lot to the writer at the time, but it meant everything to me, an exhausted single mother. Not the fact that my roses looked beautiful, but the idea that a stranger took the time to care. I still have the letter and cherish it.

If you've done all of the "right" things in your life, maybe living right before God comes easy to you. Before you were a Christian, it was possible to be nice, but you couldn't really be good. Now, because you are a Christian, you can do good things in Jesus' name. You do them not so that people call you a nice person but to glorify Jesus Christ. However, the majority of us have to stay on guard to keep the false gods from popping their little heads up if we want to do good in Jesus' name.

In his book *Being the Body*, Chuck Colson refers to churchgoers as having a consumer culture. "Spiritual consumers are interested not in what the church stands for, but in the fulfillment it can deliver," he writes.[10] Going to church to feel better. Hoping the pastor will have a positive message. Renaming the churches to be more user-friendly. That's the world's way.

When you're living in the right way, you are more interested in worshiping God and lifting up those around you than in having someone make you "feel better." True, heart-deep Christianity means that righteousness will permeate the world, society, and individuals. It means soul winning. It means that real worship is not when you're in your Sunday best but when you're in the park talking to a person who's a little less than clean, trying to show him God's love.

My husband reads his Bible and has prayer time early in the mornings in the bath. He brings me coffee in bed after that (yes, I'm spoiled). Often he tells me about whatever message he received from God that morning. Just yesterday, my unemployed son wanted some money to replace a broken cell phone. This is a huge bone of contention between me and my husband, as he feels my son should find a job and earn his own money, yet without a phone, how are employers supposed to reach him? This morning as Mickey brought me coffee, he made a disgusted face. "Okay, I had a message," he said. "I'm supposed to give him the money."

I had to laugh.

"I'm going to stop taking baths if this keeps up," he threatened.

More laughter.

But this is the kind of obedience we're supposed to have. We must make time for God and spend at least part of it listening. Often the messages we get are about helping others. Sometimes we simply need to pray for them, and sometimes the help is a little more practical. Helping people in practical ways demonstrates God's love in a way that words never can.

Please read 1 Peter 1:13.

The verse says prepare your minds for _____ .

Obedience is action. Be ready when God calls you to give money, perform a service, and yes, talk to the stinky guy in the park.

Being obedient when God gives us instructions for action is constantly an adventure. In our town, we had a period of time when there was always somebody standing in front of a certain shopping center holding up a sign: "Out of work. Please help." Often, the sign included something about a sick wife or several children to feed. Usually we laughed because the guy was well-dressed and had an expensive cell phone along with his crudely made cardboard sign.

One day I was driving out of the shopping center in a blowing, blustery snow. The young man who was holding the sign that day needed money for a bus ticket. Now, I was alone, and I try to be smart about these things. I don't stop every time because the guy could be, you know, an ax murderer, or at least a con artist. This day, however, God told me to pull over and talk to him. I glanced around to at least three other vehicles with couples, not individuals. I had to ask God, *"Why don't You send one of those couples instead of me,"* but I didn't wait for the answer. Maybe they weren't listening to Him. At any rate, it was my assignment. So I circled back around to a parking spot and motioned the fellow over to me.

He told me a sincere story that he had been working further south but the job ended, and now he was trying to hitch a ride back up to where his kids were living with his ex-wife. With enough money, he could take the bus. We spent some time talking, and I didn't feel that he was a scammer. I pulled out $25, all the cash I had in my wallet, and held it out.

"Are you sure?" he asked, having peeked into my now-empty wallet. "I don't want to take all your money."

Three more times he asked if I was sure before he would put the money in his pocket. I'm thinking, *I'm the one sitting in this nice, warm car. You are out there freezing. Take the money!*

I asked if he was a Christian. Up to this point I'm only a nice person, but I also wanted to be a witness.

"Oh, yes ma'am," he said eagerly. "I pray all the time—it's Jesus who has gotten me this far. But my Bible fell out of a hole in that backpack, so I can't read it anymore."

I already had a plan by the time I got home.

"It's completely up to you," I told my husband. "I would like for you to take him to the bus station, and I think we could give him a ticket. We certainly have an extra Bible."

Mickey's nothing if not practical. He looked up the cost of the ticket and the schedule online and agreed to do it. "I will take him to the station and buy the ticket myself," he decided.

He took the Bible I chose and drove out to the shopping center. By now the wind chill was perhaps twenty-five degrees. The man was gone. Perhaps someone gave him a ride already, or maybe he walked to a hotel. Still, we felt we had done all we were supposed to do. We were obedient and were open to God's call, and maybe that's all God wanted to see from us that day.

Please read Romans 8:14–16.

Sincere desire to do what is right before God that is of utmost importance because we are His _____ .

Please read 2 Corinthians 8:21.

They were trying to do right before both _____ and _____ .

Are you a people pleaser? If so, do you spend more of your time trying to please man than God? _____

Please read and ponder the following from *The Message*:

> Your life is a journey you must travel with a deep consciousness of God. It cost God plenty to get you out of that dead-end, empty-headed life you grew up in. He paid with Christ's sacred blood, you know. He died like an unblemished, sacrificial lamb. (1 Peter 1:18–19 MSG)

Day 3: Know Scripture

In Philippians 1:16, Paul makes a small reference to having been put "here" (in prison, in chains) for the defense of the gospel. At that time people came and spoke to Paul about Jesus, including their belief that Jesus was only one of many ways to get to God. But they were wrong, and Paul was able to correct them. Because he was at all times chained to a guard, all the guards heard this and listened to Paul's reasoning. So as he defended the gospel to others, he was also explaining it to the guards—who all began following Christ.

If you were in Paul's shoes, would you do as good a job defending the gospel? Can you explain it to a non-Christian?

_____

It is one of our greatest duties to know Scripture. Knowing it helps us love the Lord. Studying it brings us into His presence, to a place where we can hear Him speak to us. It gives us the right attitude to go on with our day. It helps us keep our focus on Christ and not on our idols.

Scripture is useful for so much more than that. Please read 2 Timothy 3:16 and list the four things this verse says Scripture is useful for:

1. _____

2. _____

3. _____

4. _____

Let's take a look at each of these uses for Scripture.

Teaching

Nothing is more beautiful than a small group that is actively teaching and learning from one another through the study of the Scripture. Whether you choose Precepts, BSF, or another small group ministry, you are choosing to live out this verse. You can trust God's Word to help you teach if you are the teacher. Likewise you can trust Him to give you a teacher who, if he or she is walking the walk, will teach you correctly.

Rebuking

To rebuke means to correct someone in a sharp way. In order to do that, you first have to know what the Bible says. When someone presents a new or different slant on God's ways, are you able to compare it with Scripture to check for truth?

Recently many television celebrities have started talking about the "many ways to God." If you know Scripture, you know this is impossible; the Bible says there is one way to God and that is through Jesus Christ. But I see Christians blindly nodding their heads at those comments and repeating what has been said as, well, gospel.

It drives me nuts.

While many people say that you can strip all religions down to their core and reveal a fundamental likeness, there is one drastic difference between Christianity and other religions. No matter which denomination of Christianity you participate in, we're all in the same boat. The people in the other boats all have to perform in order to receive a blessing from God. They have to give alms, or follow a certain diet, or perform certain deeds. They have to pray a specific number of times in a special way.

In our faith, Jesus is God reaching out to us in relationship. It doesn't matter if we prayed six times today or not. He's still reaching. He's reaching out in love so much that He volunteered to be a substitute for our wrongdoing. We have the only faith that can say that.

Suppose you had an illness, and the doctor told you there was only one cure. It's a simple cure, but it's the only one. Let's say the cure is drinking apple juice every day for a week. But you don't care for apple juice. It's boring and narrow-minded. Your friends would probably make fun of you if they knew you were drinking apple juice. So you decide to drink orange juice instead.

The next week you return to the doctor, and to his surprise you're still sick.

"I told you how to cure it," he says. "Why didn't you follow my instructions?"

Every one of us really is sick, and our illness is sin. We can't make it go away by ignoring it or by doing good deeds. Good people and bad people all suffer from the same level of this sickness, and it's terminal. Only the Great Physician is able to heal it with His simple cure.

The point is, if you don't know Scripture, then you won't know when it is being taken out of context, twisted, or misquoted. You could end up following the orange juice cure, when what you need is apple juice. That's dangerous to you and your family—and it makes room for idols.

On a scale of 1–10, how well do you know Scripture? _____

If your number is high—congratulations! If it is low, what can you do to change it?

_____

_____

While it is important to know Scripture, read and study it, you don't have to have the whole Bible memorized to use it for comparison. There are tons of resources. I'll bet your Bible probably even has a concordance right in the back, where you can look up verses by topic. Or use a search engine. I often visit Google and type in the part of a verse I know, and it brings up the chapter and verse number.

Correction

Sometimes it is not strangers or the media that present wrong ideas, but friends or even church leaders. Topics that could fall under this category run the gamut from small misinterpretations of Scripture up to chronic sin that must be dealt with firmly and fast.

It is hard when we know that our closest friends need to hear a difficult message. But as a real-deal Christian, a loving friend in this journey, you can deliver that message with truth and grace. If it is appropriate, offer to become an accountability partner for a period of time.

A true Christian friend (are you one?) will build up the other spiritually, emotionally, and physically. Friends help each other receive encouragement and strength through talking and listening. We think that we share friendship because it feels good, but godly friendships are also commanded. Proverbs 27:17 says, "As iron sharpens iron, so one person sharpens another."

It is even more difficult if the person in the wrong is in a leadership position. But as part of the loving family of God, I believe it is our duty to guard our church and its positions diligently. Don't allow for corruption, and don't sit by thinking someone else will take care of it. Just as Peter was a rock, each of us is responsible for being a solid rock within our congregation, our community of believers.

Sometimes the person who is wrong will be you. I just hate that, don't you? But none of us are perfect, so it will happen. When it does, admit it and offer a sincere apology with as much grace as you can muster. I remember once when I was upset with a family member, and I finally voiced how hurt I was. The man dragged out his voice in the most grudging, sarcastic tone, "Well if I have to, I'll do my Christian duty and apologize."

Was that the apology? I'm really not sure. There wasn't much sincerity, and that's why I still remember it so clearly nearly thirty years later.

Training in Righteousness

We are saved by grace, but we are still sinners. That means we continually need training in righteousness. We hear the Word, study it, and apply it. We hear it again and learn something new that we didn't know. We study a little more about it. We apply it again. Wash, rinse, repeat.

And of course we train the little ones to cultivate right minds and proper morals. We must raise children in the church surrounded by godly people. In this way they become exposed not only to your careful training but also to what Jesus can do and has done for them and others. What an awesome way to grow up.

Day 4: Care for Your Heart

OU CAN LEARN ALMOST ALL you need to know about caring for your heart and protecting it from idols in Proverbs 4. Please read that chapter now.

It is a strange truth that we have to dig for understanding of biblical truth. It doesn't come with birth, IQ, or salvation. Rather, a deeper understanding is achieved over time by studying God's Word.

In his book *Loved by God*, Bishop T. D. Jakes says, "God often withholds blessing and prosperity from us for a season in order to temper our character or to correct flawed behavior. Then, when the blessing comes, we will be mature enough to handle it."[11]

This is the sort of understanding we must develop. Of course, we'll never understand all of God's ways, but if we don't get the basic concepts, we could easily become discouraged or lose faith that He will answer our prayers. Years ago our country was steeped in faith and hope, but now it is easy to find people who have no hope. They have no overarching life story of promises and meaning. By developing a godly understanding, we will continue to have hope and faith. We'll realize that God does everything in His own time—and His timetable doesn't match ours.

Read verses 5–9 in Proverbs 4 again. These verses tell us we must place value on wisdom and discernment. You know how some families place more importance on some things than others, say, sports? Or musical training?

Proverbs 4 tells us that wisdom and discernment are the things of utmost importance. By pursuing them we will wear _____ and _____ . (Your answers may vary depending on the translation used.)

Verses 10–13 implore us to *stick with it*. For some people, sticking with a plan is a really difficult task. I was just reading an Internet article by Pam Young, author of *Sidetracked*

Home Executives. Though the article is about housework,[12] the same thing could be said about our journey with God.

She said that many of us get the plan in place, then quit. How many times have we said, "I'm going to read the whole Bible this year," and then we don't? How often have you resolved to pray every day, then seven days later you realize you've missed five days? It's because we don't think it's fun, according to Pam. We *have to* instead of *want to.* So the trick is to make it fun. I don't know about you, but the thought of going to heaven is fun enough for me. The excitement of bringing others to Jesus, the joy we will have when we get there, pales everything else by comparison.

Do you have the "want to" enough to stick with your plan?

_____

If not, what steps can you take to change that?

_____

_____

_____

Verses 14–19 (please reread those now) talk a lot about paths. Avoid bad company and choose the straight road. I have heard at least twenty times in the past few days that there are always choices. It seems everyone is talking about it. Choosing the straight road is not always easy and not even always clear. But choosing that road keeps us where we want to be.

Choosing that road means we will turn from evil. As your spiritual eyes are wide open, diligently guarding your heart against idols, it is also wise to avoid isolation or prolonged separation from your Christian family, your church family. These people help us make sure we're actually on the straight road.

Please read verses 20–27 now. These are the heart of the Proverbs 4. In fact, I have an entire speech I give on just these verses. They tell us to keep:

» your mouth _____ ,

» your eyes _____ ,

» and your feet _____ .

By following the instruction in Proverbs 4, we can contend for the Word—without ugliness or dissention. We can get down to the business of saving the lost. Remember that for the righteous, light increases. For others, darkness remains. Righteousness brings you health and life. But you must have right living *and* doctrine—both.

Day 5: Celebrate and Review

I TAUGHT VIOLIN LESSONS FOR OVER twenty-five years. Whenever my students reached the end of a lesson book, it was cause for celebration. They had reached a new level of learning. But before we moved forward, we spent a couple of weeks playing back through their "old" material together. We smiled at the places they used to make mistakes, where now the music flowed freely. They were always eager to share their favorite pieces just one more time before moving on.

Like those students, you've finished the course—congratulations! So today I'd like for you to do what my students often did: use today as a review day. Go back over the study. Savor the messages you received from God. (I hope you wrote them in your book!) Reread the highlighted parts and the notes you wrote into the study. Consider memorizing or writing out the most important parts to post where you can see them. Enjoy the process just once more before you put it away.

Hopefully your heart has changed over these few weeks. I know mine has. And now we no longer have to call our heart an idol factory. There's a new definition: my heart is a fortress where God and I exist together.

May God bless you, and may you continue to grow in knowledge and truth!

Tanya Logan
Email: tanyawriter@gmail.com
Website: www.tanyalogan.com
Twitter: @tanyawriter

LEADER'S GUIDE

Come Back to Jesus—
And Don't Bring Your Blackberry

*N*OTE TO GROUP LEADERS: THESE are my own notes from preparing to lead the class myself. This guide is merely a set of ideas, *not rules*—feel free to use it or not. During the focus group sessions, I could only talk for about five to ten minutes before the group took over, discussing the lesson and sharing ideas. This usually lasted to the end of the hour.

Week 1

*M*Y PRAYER FOR MY FOCUS group was Philippians 1:9–11 during the first two weeks. I actually emailed them all and told them. It's powerful to know someone has your back as you embark on a new study in the Word.

Housekeeping Rules

» Absolutely no phones!

» What is said here stays here. We observe complete confidentiality out of respect for one another.
» Prayer requests should be for each other and immediate family only. No Internet stories, etc.

Let's Begin

About me, the leader. *It is important for the leader to gain the respect of the group, to "earn" the right to lead them through this journey. Tell a little about yourself. Share your own idol experiences, where appropriate.*

Open with Prayer
Discussion Time

Ask: What is an idol? (Wait for responses)

The book's definition: whatever repeatedly gets between you and your worship of God. Other possible responses: Something that we set our heart on. What demands full devotion or ultimate commitment. It is valuable to you. It is repeatedly front and center. You would feel lost if you lost it.

An idol is:

» what we (wrongly) love, trust, and/or obey
» whatever inspires or persuades us
» what influences and/or holds dominion over us
» where we put our faith
» what we revere or fear
» how we serve

Read or have someone read: Psalm 63:1–4

That's where we want to be. These are the words of someone who has been in God's presence. He has tasted the spiritual beauty and wants to be present in God's glory again.

Ask:

What has David discovered about God's love (v. 3)?
What is his response (v. 4)?

Introduce Week 1

Idols are the most discussed topic in the Bible but the least addressed today. Sixty-three percent of us are casual Christians. Casual: doesn't care about idols; not in pursuit of a relationship with God.

If you'll stick it out with me for these next six weeks, we'll clear out some of the "stuff" so you find more time to spend with God. First we have to figure out whether any of that stuff is idols.

Let's get started! (Before ending this introductory meeting on the first week, encourage your group to work through the five days of each week before attending the next week's group meeting, so they will be prepared for discussion together.)

At End

If you want to enter God's presence, go to Him in prayer. He wants to come to you, love you, and refresh you. Like David, you can remember by recording your times in a notebook when God seemed near, when you felt blessed.

It builds faith to write about who Jesus is and who you are in Him. In Him you will have confidence to approach the throne of God and root out these pesky idols.

Close with Prayer

Week 2

Open with Prayer Requests and Prayer
Introduce New Class Members
Let's Begin

Go over week 1, and allow sharing from members.

Further Discussion

Read or have someone read Philippians 2:14–18.

Do everything without grumbling. I (Tanya) am a Southern Baptist, and we've made grumbling an art form. Speaking of grumbling, my Aunt Marti died during the weeks I was leading this Bible study for the first time. She had a very difficult life and *never* grumbled, always choosing to rejoice and share joy. And her Bible reading. I can't seem to keep up with a "through the Bible in one year" study. When I gathered all the items from Marti's Bible, I discovered her group is doing it in ninety days! And the day she died, in addition to working a full shift and attending Sunday evening services, she'd checked off her Bible reading for the day. I will never grumble again. Promise.

Introduce Week 2

Week 2 is about drifting. Members may mention that drifting is not an idol. Drift is not an idol in and of itself, but it *leads to* false gods and busyness in the wrong kind of things. Drift lets Satan sneak in. That's why it has a place in an idol study.

Our obligation as a church society is to be "in one spirit." That means we have to have love for each other and unity.

Ask: Do we love enough?

When people within our church family are drifting, that unity falls apart. Paul's letter to the Philippians appeals to that, and he asks them conditionally:

» if you have any encouragement in Christ
» if you draw comfort from His love
» if you have fellowship with the Spirit
» if you have any tenderness and compassion

. . . *then* love each other, agree with each other, be deep-spirited friends. Put yourself aside. Help others get ahead. Forget yourself long enough to lend a helping hand.

It doesn't matter if you have everything your heart desires, or if you feel lonely and unwanted. If God is not the ultimate thing, you will grab for false gods. Obedience is the key to experience a satisfying relationship with God and the richness of His holy presence. He knows the depths of our hearts. He knows who is on the verge of drift. He feels our pain. He hears our cries. Are you brave enough to obey, and then wait for Him to do the rest?

Close with Prayer

Week 3

Open with Prayer Requests and Prayer
Let's Begin

Go over week 2, and allow sharing from members.

Further Discussion

Ask: What is the most important thing you learned this week?

Challenge class members: If you thought of anyone who is drifting, commit to pray for them for five days.

Introduce Week 3

A week without . . . something. *Leaders: you don't know what your group members will be without. It's an extremely personal choice. Pray that God leads them to see what they need to be without this week. This is our most difficult week of the study.*

Please read or have someone read:

Romans 12:1–2

2 Corinthians 3:18

Jesus did not run around from place to place. Remember in Matthew when the disciples tried to rush Him past the children and He refused to be hurried? He was not performance based.

We need to learn to serve the Lord without distraction. Satan will try to redirect our focus.

Discuss what group members might give up for the week. Be sure to have an idea of your own, or some example ideas.

Close with Prayer

Week 4

Open with Prayer Requests and prayer
Let's Begin

Leaders: Expect a lot of discussion today! I like to talk about the "Myth of Mom" first, then end with a discussion of their week without their false gods—so they can talk as long as they need to—but you can also reverse the order so the order remains consistent.

The Myth of Mom

There are two myths in popular culture that if bought into can keep mothers trapped on a treadmill going nowhere.

Myth #1: Mothers can do everything well. No, we cannot. God never told us to do everything well. He said that whatever we do, do it all for the glory of God (see 1 Corinthians 10:31). The more God has a say in our activities and schedules, the more we will be able to do all to God's glory.

Myth #2: Mothers can make everyone like and approve of them. We will never, no matter how hard we try, become all things to all people in our lives. To try eventually makes everyone miserable. Moses' father-in-law, Jethro, phrased it beautifully when he saw his son-in-law's vain attempt: "What you are doing is not good. You and these people who come to you will only wear yourselves out" (Exodus 18:17–18).

Ask: Sound familiar?

Just as God had primary responsibilities for Moses, God has them for you and me. We will wear ourselves out if we become enslaved to the needs and desires of others.

Please read Galatians 1:10.

Please read 2 Corinthians 3:18.

Ask: If the main thing is to cheerfully please God, what in your life is *not* the main thing? In the 2 Corinthians verse, it talks about our ever-increasing transformation. Is there anything that is holding you back from being transformed?

Further Discussion

Go over week 3, and allow sharing from members about their results of living without something.

Introduce Week 4

During this week without your idol you likely experienced many emotions—ranging from fear and insecurity, especially at first, to I hope the beginnings of a different type of peace and freedom, and more time to spend with your Creator. Because it's been a difficult week, during week 4 of this study, we will concentrate on what it means to spend time with Jesus, and the promises that brings to our lives. Jesus called His followers to be constantly committed to Him, as branches to the Vine. Yet even in the loving arms of our Lord, we may have to be pruned of whatever might get in the way of that relationship with Him. As we continue to hold fast to God, His gentle hands will prune us, bring more growth and security in Him, and give us joy in life, even when we walk through valleys.

Close with Prayer

Week 5

Open with Prayer Requests and Prayer
Let's Begin

Go over week 4, and allow sharing from members.

Further Discussion

Talk about being cleaned versus being pruned by Jesus (from day 2). Ask: Do you recognize when He is cleaning or pruning you? Does that make it easier to bear?

Talk about security. Ask class members to look at day 3 in their book and share what they wrote down about security or insecurity.

At the end of week 4, readers were invited to read some or all of the following verses:

John 3:16–17
John 13:6–9
John 15:13
1 Peter 5:7
Galatians 5:22–24
1 Corinthians 13

Invite them to share the ones they felt especially connected with.

Introduce Week 5

Do you know who you are in Christ? Do you understand His plans for you?

If you are a person without much self-confidence, you may not have realized that a Christian's confidence is actually Christ-confidence. What a relief to know we can be confident in Him, because He is the only one who is perfect.

We may still be struggling with false gods. We may have removed one only to find there are others. Praise God that He will always lovingly show us where mistakes are made. Thank Him that He is so patient with each of us.

Close with Prayer

Week 6

Open with Prayer Requests and Prayer
Let's Begin

Go over week 5, and allow sharing from members.

Further Discussion

Read the following from week 5, day 4: "Where do you put your trust? Do you trust your husband? Your pastor? Your best friend? Do you trust God with all your heart?"

Please read Hebrews 11:6.

Ask: How do we learn to trust God?

Daily Bible study and prayer are the only ways to develop faith and trust. We must trust Him completely. I find if there is some area where I'm not trusting, God tests me on it, which brings it to my attention.

Introduce Week 6

Week 6, the final lesson, is about remaining idol free. Remember that just because we've cleared out one false god doesn't mean others won't try to sneak in! Be prepared. Be "prayed up." Be on guard.

Leaders: You'll want to decide whether to have a seventh week, a wrapping-up meeting of your six-week study. There may not be time in the schedule. You may want to have it at someone's house instead of in the church building.

Close with Prayer

Week 7

Open with Prayer Requests and Prayer
Let's Begin

Go over week 6. *Leaders*: Week 6 is more about Christian living than idols. But right living is the key to idol prevention. It's like an anti-idol spray. Ask members to follow along in their book, where they have probably already filled in the following blanks.

Please read John 14:27.

A real Christian experiences ——————————————————— .

Please read Matthew 5:8.

A real Christian strives for _____.

Please read Proverbs 3:5–6.

The real Christian obeys, because he has _____ in God.

Please read 1 John 4:7–11.

The real Christian has _____.

Further Discussion

As we move forward, let's also consider Proverbs 4:
Read Proverbs 4:11–12 and discuss.
Read Proverbs 4:13–15 and discuss.
Read Proverbs 4:16–19 and discuss.

Remember, God can:
» *deliver* whatever we ask in His name;
» *delay* to fit His perfect timing (only He sees the end from the beginning);
» *deny* and say no because we ask amiss; or give a
» *different* and better answer.

Pray: "Lord, help me to be patient and persistent . . . and leave the answers to my prayers in Your hands."

Close with Prayer

FEEDBACK FORM

*L*EADERS: IF YOU USE THE feedback form below, I would love for you to share your results with me at Tanyawriter@gmail.com.

Come Back to Jesus Survey

Please rate each question on a scale of 1–10, with 1 being "totally disagree" and 10 being "completely agree."

I found the class interesting.

    2   3   4   5   6   7   8   9   10

The material was relevant to my life.

    2   3   4   5   6   7   8   9   10

There was too much homework.

    2   3   4   5   6   7   8   9   10

There was not enough homework.

    2   3   4   5   6   7   8   9   10

The study was too easy.

       2   3   4   5   6   7   8   9   10

The study was too hard.

       2   3   4   5   6   7   8   9   10

I would recommend this class to a friend.

       2   3   4   5   6   7   8   9   10

Comments:

ENDNOTES

1. Timothy C. Morgan, "Porn's Stranglehold, *Inside CT.* Posted March 7, 2008. *Christianity Today: www.christianitytoday.com/ct/2008/march/20.7.html* (January 2, 2013).

2. "Addiction." *Dictionary.com, unabridged, based on the Random House Dictionary,* © *Random House, Inc. 2013: http://dictionary.reference.com/browse/addiction?s=t* (January 4, 2013).

3. "Initiative." *Dictionary.com: http://dictionary.reference.com/browse/initiative?s=t* (January 2, 2013).

4. *The Sabbath Recorder,* **vol. 84, American Sabbath Tract Society, Jan. 7, 1918, 572.**

5. James I. Packer, *Your Father Loves You: Daily Insights for Knowing God* (Wheaton, Ill.: Harold Shaw, 1986), April 19.

6. C. J. Mahaney, ed., *Worldliness: Resisting the Seduction of a Fallen World* (Wheaton, Ill.: Crossway, 2008).

7. "Gossip." Last updated December 30, 2012. *Wikipedia: http://en.wikipedia.org/wiki/Gossip* (January 3, 2013).

8. "Hope." *Thesaurus.com,* http://thesaurus.com/browse/hope?s=t (January 3, 2013).

9. Mark Twain, *Notebook, 1894. Twainquotes.com: http://www.twainquotes.com/Truth.html* (January 4, 2013).

10. Charles Colson and Ellen Vaughn, *Being the Body: A New Call for the Church to Be Light in the Darkness.* (Nashville: Thomas Nelson, 2003), 23.

11. T. D. Jakes, *Loved by God* (Dallas, TX: Albury, 2000), 12.

12. Pam Young, "Still Disorganized? I Know Why!" May 31, 2012. *Make It Fun and It Will Get Done: http://www.makeitfunanditwillgetdone.com/2012/05/still-disorganized-i-know-why/* (January 3, 2013).